Creating Growth from Change

3

Creating Growth from Change

HOW YOU REACT,

DEVELOP AND GROW

Rupert Eales-White

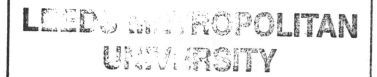
The McGraw-Hill Companies

London · New York · St Louis · San Francisco · Auckland
Bogotá · Caracas · Lisbon · Madrid · Mexico
Milan · Montreal · New Delhi · Panama · Paris · San Juan
São Paulo · Singapore · Sydney · Tokyo · Toronto

Published by
McGraw-Hill Publishing Company
Shoppenhangers Road, Maidenhead, Berkshire SL6 2QL, England
Telephone 01628 23432
Fax 01628 770224

British Library Cataloguing in Publication Data
Eales-White, Rupert
  Creating growth from change: how you react, develop and
  grow
  1. Organizational change   2. Success in business
  I. Title
  658.4'06

  ISBN 0-07-709347-X

Library of Congress Cataloging-in-Publication Data
Eales-White, Rupert.
    Creating growth from change: how you react, develop and grow /
  Rupert Eales-White.
      p.   cm.
    Includes bibliographical references and index.
    ISBN 0-07-709347-X
      1. Organizational change—Management. 2. Change (Psychology)
  I. Title.
  HD58.8.E15   1994
  658.4'06–dc20   94-18935
                                                               CIP

McGraw-Hill

A Division of The **McGraw-Hill** Companies

12345 BL 9876

Typeset by BookEns Ltd., Royston, Herts.
and printed and bound in Great Britain
by Biddles Ltd., Guildford, Surrey

Printed on permanent paper in compliance with ISO Standard 9706

Contents

Preface

Expectations

Many of you are busy, pragmatic people, who demand value for money. You may accept a little theory, some research, anecdotes, etc., but what is important is whether you receive a satisfactory answer to the 'so what?' questions; for example, 'So what does this theory mean in practical terms?' 'So what use can I make of it in the real world?', 'So what can I do to ensure I get growth, when reacting to or initiating change?'

This book aims to produce recipes that you can follow, if they make sense for you. But the book does more.

Sir John Whitmore, a former European and British car rally champion and now writer and practitioner on coaching, was talking with a group of executives on a programme I was running a few months ago. He drew two pictures on a flip chart. The key feature of the first was a large, empty, container or vessel. Near the top of this vessel, on the outside, was a jug of water to be poured into the vessel. As time passed, it was suggested, different people with different jugs of water filled up the container.

This represented the *empty vessel* view of humanity, believed in down the years both by educationalists and psychologists and permeating our cultural approach to 'learning'. The approach is based on the fact of ignorance, which holds when we are young and in many adult situations. It assumes that we learn by being told—by receiving guidance, instruction or command (the language varies on how soft or hard we see things).

Certainly, it is the conventional way most of us are educated in a series of relationships down the years—parent and child, teacher and pupil, lecturer and student, boss and subordinate. There is a little interaction, with the expert transmitter sending the information and knowledge to the passive receiver.

Incidentally, this approach is also at the heart of many cultures, which treat their employees as children, and we shall discuss this further in Chapters 1 and 9.

The core of Sir John's second picture was an acorn, from which were growing a few leaves. This was the *acorn* view of humanity. Here we are seen as acorns, and if we receive the right nourishment, and are supported and helped, we shall grow into giant oak trees, standing tall, confident and competent. But for acorns, truth and knowledge come from within. We just need the right environment in which to grow.

Teachers *give* us the answers. Coaches *ask* us difficult questions that force us to find the answers for ourselves. Teachers *impart* knowledge; coaches *promote* learning through self-discovery, recognizing that we know much more than we think we know.

We can be comfortable with teaching, and uncomfortable with coaching. Growth comes from discomfort—making mistakes and learning from them.

This dichotomy, however, is too black and white. There is never one right answer. Sometimes we want, and need, to be treated as 'empty vessels'. If we are in an unfamiliar situation—say, a new role beyond our current expertise—we want some guidance; we need to be told what we should do and why. If we receive no guidance and are left to sink or swim, we may drown despite the fact that we could have been Olympic champions if only we had been taught how to swim.

However, when we are competent and confident in our role, the last thing we want or need is a boss telling us what to do.

So horses for courses.

This book recognizes the value of teaching *and* coaching. So I shall not simply provide models, theories and recipes, but shall also ask you difficult questions. I shall ask you to invest time and emotion, so that you can, if you so desire, discover the recipe that is right for you.

Purpose and background

The purpose of this book is to enable you to create growth out of change, whether it is change that is imposed when you are in a reactive mode, or change that you initiate in a proactive mode. The potential for growth is always there, but all too often growth is limited or even negative. The latter is inevitable in the short term when we react to significant, sudden change, which is perceived as negative, e.g. redundancy.

We all live in a world of change, and while this book concentrates on our business lives, it also considers some of the many changes in our personal lives—particularly events in our past, even childhood, that have affected our current capacity to gain personal growth.

Looking at our working lives, the nation and its citizens have experienced considerable change and associated uncertainty. For some, it has been very traumatic, e.g. loss of job. For many others, there have been a host of changes, often compressed into a very short period of time.

As someone whose job it is to help managers and executives from a wide range of companies and industries to try to grow and develop against a backcloth of change, I have experienced or learned about and discussed many of the changes that have occurred or are taking place. The list is long. Some items on the list are:

- seeing others lose their jobs

- unsure of own future

- new roles and responsibilities

- new objectives and targets

- a much wider span of control

- new IT systems

- cost-cutting

- reduction in the tangible and intangible benefits of employment

- stress at a higher level than encountered before

- new mission, vision or values, with a drive to a new culture

- quality improvement programmes

- new structures and systems

- sudden, unexpected promotion

- company makes losses for first time

- significant increase in the flattening of the organization and the emergence of the 'plateaued' manager

- rapid growth and profitability, leading to overheating and overwork.

Some managers I know have experienced many of these changes in less than a year! For most, the changes have been imposed, but some have been the initiators. Where individuals have been involved in taking decisions that affect them personally, the ability to gain growth rather than pain has increased.

This is a recurring reality. Most of us want to contribute towards creating the recipe and cooking the cake we have to eat.

While time is given in the book to considering significant change, I also look at all the little changes that we experience quite frequently, such as:

- criticism or praise

- requests from our boss

- being presented with a *fait accompli*
- being late for an important meeting
- being flattered and imposed upon
- a proposal or idea from a subordinate
- interruptions
- a rude client.

Structure and content

As already mentioned, this book has a dual purpose: to transfer knowledge of how to get personal growth out of change *and* to enable you to actually get more growth than is currently the case through exploration, discovery, reflection and action. It is structured accordingly.

The first chapter introduces the themes developed in subsequent chapters, providing both an organizational and individual perspective. We look at the dimensions of change and the key dilemma change creates. We also look at exactly how we can create an approach for ourselves, which will guarantee maximum personal growth—considering the difference between learning and teaching, and how we can follow the *learning cycle* and climb the *learning ladder*.

Then I turn to you, the individual, and ask you to complete a simple self-assessment to establish whether you have a particular orientation or preference towards change. I call the four approaches, which combine to produce the profile:

- LOGICAL DETACHED (LD)
- NEGATIVE CONTROL (NC)
- PEOPLE FOCUSED (PF)
- POSITIVE CREATIVE (PC)

Each approach is explained, as is the derivation. Meaning is developed by interpreting six profiles of actual individuals both in absolute terms and compared to the normal or average profile.

We then move on from discovery to reflection. I ask you, through a series of structured questions, to analyse, reflect on and distil learning from some historic change that you experienced, which had a major impact on your thinking and feeling. Again, we consider five experiences of others, focusing on business situations at this stage. Personal experiences are covered in Chapter 5.

Next we look at the concept of the four development levels: *survival, security, self-esteem* and *growth*. At a moment of time, or over time, we may be at one level of development. Which level it is will have a major impact on our capacity to get growth out of change. I also look briefly at leadership, that vital role many of us have in our working environments. I connect leadership to development level and highlight the impact leadership has on other people's capacity to gain growth from change.

The next chapter considers how we react to change. We discuss the likely impact on our development level; how we can control reactions; and how we can move into a positive growth phase (when the change is perceived negatively initially) sooner rather than later by constructively intervening in the natural cycle.

I then consider the interaction of the individual with others on a one-to-one basis, whether persuading others to change or helping them through change. Again, there is an assessment with a difference. I ask you first to consider how you persuade or influence others and to build your own profile. I ask you then to select a colleague with whom you work closely, preferably an individual who reports directly to you. He or she should complete a questionnaire which determines that person's perception of how you influence and persuade. The questionnaire is structured so that this individual will not know what the answers mean. Only you will be able to score the profile, derive meaning and compare it with your self-portrait. This is powerful, as it identifies the gaps in perception. It is practical, as it gives you the chance, proactively, to manage change for the better—to improve the quality of a business relationship *and* obtain personal growth.

Developing skills forms the content of the next chapter. I look at practical ways, both organizationally and individually, of increasing the flow of ideas, and then consider how we can close gaps between behavioural intention and impact, promote discovery and manage expectations and perceptions.

Next I consider the team, and how a leader can create growth from the team, with particular focus on change within a team, whether in members or task. Finally, I look at the organizational level, considering how organizations have created and can create a culture that is positive to change and how they manage the process successfully. The focus is on the top executives of organizations: the people with the power to deny or create the environment where individuals, teams and the organization itself can create growth out of change.

I hope you find the book provocative, challenging, relevant and helpful. Using the book as a catalyst as well as a conventional read, it is not a truism to say that the more you put in, the more you will get out.

Rupert Eales-White

Acknowledgements

To my wife Jessie for her support and help; Chantal Garner for her efficient process management and chart production; my colleagues, managers and executives, who completed questionnaires; and Edward de Bono, Roger Harrison, Ned Hermann, Sir Andrew Pettigrew and Sir John Whitmore for their powerful contributions to the concepts in the book.

Change and learning

> *Change is the law of life. Those, who look*
> *only to the past or present, are certain to*
> *miss the future.*
>
> JOHN F. KENNEDY

Introduction

Change is '*making or becoming different*'. We start by looking at the dimensions of change: at how we can characterize change by different factors or variables, each of which has a range or dimension. Next we consider the key dilemma change poses. This dilemma occurs because the way we respond (organizationally or individually) to the uncertainty produced by change can and does clash with the way we respond to the unpredictable nature of the outcomes of change. Finally we look at how we can achieve real growth through learning. In the process, many of the themes and concepts are introduced, which will be developed in subsequent chapters.

Dimensions of change

The factors and dimensions of change are set out in Table 1.1. Let us look at each factor in turn.

Environment

It is important to recognize the environment or context in which change occurs, as that is a significant variable we have to appreciate and manage if we are going to gain growth. The environment can be stable, where change has been absent, or one in which change has become the norm.

Many employees in many organizations have experienced change in recent years. In fact every manager and executive I have asked 'Is your business environment one of stability or change?' has replied 'change'.

Table 1.1 Dimensions of change

Factor or variable	Dimension	
Environment	Stable ———————→	Change
Continuity	Connected with present/past ——→	Disconnected
Size	Insignificant ————————→	Significant
Phasing	Gradual ————————→	Sudden
Frequency	Once —————————→	Repeated
Duration	Short —————————→	Long
Initiator	Self —————————→	Others
Development level	Survival ————————→	Growth
Perception	Negative ————————→	Positive
Expectation	Expected ————————→	Unexpected
Impact	Shallow ————————→	Deep
	Temporary ————————→	Permanent

Additionally, every manager or executive from a company formed 10 or more years ago has stated that the pace of change has accelerated in the last five years in comparison with the previous five years.

Repeated change produces a positive or negative mindset. If organizations approach change with too much control, too much logical cost-cutting, too much regulation and procedure, and too many new structures and systems, their employees find themselves endlessly in reactive rather than proactive mode. Their perceptions of change are negative. There is increasing resistance or sullen acquiescence.

As mentioned in the Preface, there are organizations that have restructured, refocused their markets, de-layered, introduced quality initiatives and major new IT systems, and given those employees who have not been sacked new roles and responsibilities, 'impossible targets' and new appraisal systems *all more or less at the same time*.

That is not the way to manage change for growth, as evidenced by research into organizational change, details of which are set out in Chapter 9, 'Growing the organization'.

Nevertheless, human beings show an amazing capacity to be continuously thrown off balance, and come through smiling—a mixture of grit, integrity, client and organizational loyalty.

Where organizations create a culture of creativity and employee involvement, a positive attitude results. A positive experience of change leads to a positive approach to change, which leads to an increased probability of the next experience being positive.

Vicious and virtuous circles!

Whether we obtain growth individually or organizationally often depends on whether we ask the right question. The question we tend to focus on is:

'What should we do differently to respond to change?'

This is a very logical question. Explicit in the definition of change is *difference*. If all our business environments are changing, then we must do different things to what we have been doing. We know with a high level of confidence that continuation of past best practice guarantees failure in the future, as the one future we can predict not taking place under change is that generated through extrapolating the past. So we must ask the question.

It is quite an unimportant question in the sense that any group of intelligent, experienced employees could reply with very good answers. What is more, the answers would not be very different for different groups of employees. The much more important question is:

'How do we ensure that we gain agreement to what needs to be done differently and it is carried through?'

The second question often receives less conscious, strategic thought by decision takers than the first.

Put simply, process is more important than task. Let us take an example:

A few years ago a core division of a large UK insurance company recognized that, if it was going to continue in business, it had to make fundamental changes both to its customer base and the way the products and services were distributed.

The divisional board met frequently over a period of months to decide exactly what needed to be done. Eventually, they had developed a complete strategic action plan. They were about to start the implementation ball rolling using a wide range of communications when it was stopped in its tracks by the simple question of a junior member: 'Well, we know exactly what needs to be done, but *we* are not going to implement our strategy. How are we going to ensure that it is implemented effectively?'

The board spent some time considering this question and came up with a very effective answer. They flew the top 160 senior managers, responsible for implementing their strategy, to a hotel in Europe for a weekend and presented them with the problems they, the board, had identified and all the information they had gleaned, *but not* the solutions!

Over the weekend, using a group approach, the managers came up with a strategic response, which was almost identical to the one the board had devised. Not surprisingly the board accepted their own strategy! More importantly, the implementation was effective.

Part of the implementation meant redundancy, including some of the senior managers!

CASE STUDY

Therefore:

■ In a world of change, asking the right question is more important than finding the 'right' answer. 'Right' answers can be wrong, because they may answer the wrong question.

■ 'Change' means changing our attitude to risk. We must be prepared to take risks that we would not normally contemplate. The board were, in their minds, taking a big risk, as the senior managers could have suggested something completely different.

If the environment is one where change is the norm, so that we are dealing with change on change, then we need to determine whether the current climate is negative or positive. If it is negative, we shall need to rethink our whole strategy towards change management itself, and how we can alter the process to alter the mentality. If it is positive, it is simply a question of ensuring that we maintain the status quo (i.e. a positive attitude) when introducing the change.

The problem is different if change is taking place where there was stability in the past. This is not the case today, but was for many of our companies and industries in earlier decades. The main problem here is lack of recognition of the need for change and the nature and direction of change. The result is the application of such solutions as cost-cutting, which worked before, but cannot succeed where the underlying dynamics and success factors in the marketplace have altered. In such situations, it is important to generate a perception of crisis to overcome inertia, and to ensure recognition of the need for change.

Continuity

A change can connect or not connect to the present and past. It can represent a discontinuity. If it does, it is more difficult to manage, even if it is 'good news'. We all know stories of pools winners (and how many of us fantasize about winning the pools?), where this seemingly highly pleasant event has destroyed their lives. There is no connection to the past, assuming the winners were not already wealthy. The event is outside their existing model of reality, and therefore they have no 'learned' means of guiding themselves into the new future.

As we shall see when we consider some of the responses to the questionnaire in Chapter 3, it is always those abrupt changes, where there has been a lack of continuity, that cause the greatest reaction and are the most difficult to manage.

This has two implications for managing change for growth, whether within an organization or in an individual.

Recognize value

Don't throw out the baby with the bath water. There is always a richness and value in the past. Seek it out and build it in to any changes you make. This has a dual benefit—it makes the changes more effective *and* more acceptable.

This was brought home forcefully to me, when in a strategic planning role for Barclays Bank. We got carried away with scanning the future and failed to connect to the past, until we were told that we could not sell such a future, and others had trod in part the trail we thought we were blazing. We should study the maps they had already produced.

Many managers and executives, when taking on a new role, make changes straight away. This may stem from the need to prove themselves, to stamp their authority and make their mark and/or because they must show themselves to be better than their predecessors, and the way to do that is to be different from them.

Equally, many mangers and executives practise what they refer to as the 100 day rule—do nothing and listen for the first 100 days in a new job. Then they recognize the worth and value of approaches and methods, which they instinctively wanted to change, and the changes they make are better, as they are built on solid ground.

Manage perception

Perception is reality. So if we can build a perception of continuity by creating connection or stressing the connection that exists, we shall produce more acceptance than if we emphasize, consciously or otherwise, just how different things are going to be in our brave new world. This is particularly true when we are introducing change into an environment of change *and* if we want to create a continuous improvement culture.

Like all rules, there is an exception. As mentioned in the previous section, if there is organizational or individual inertia we have to create a perception of crisis to overcome it. There needs to be a jolt to the system.

When Brian Pitman was made managing director of Lloyds Bank in 1983, Lloyds was trading at a discount to net asset value and was the most vulnerable of the clearing banks to takeover.

Brian Pitman deliberately exaggerated this threat and communicated it widely to provide the necessary jolt to the system. Lloyds Bank has for a number of years been the most profitable bank with a premium rating in the marketplace.

In 1983, the Bank of England would not have permitted the takeover of Lloyds Bank!

Size

How significant or 'large' a change is will have an important bearing on its impact on us and our ability to cope, then grow. In the area of aggression, a sharp word is a fairly small change. A heavy blow with a hammer is a rather significant event.

This book looks at little, insignificant changes as well as large, significant changes.

Good project management is based on breaking the project down into manageable components, bound by interim deadlines. The same holds for good change management.

Phasing

How the change is phased in is an important variable. It is generally true that if change is phased in gradually, it is more successful and there is more growth than if it is suddenly implemented. This is simply because there can be gradual adjustment of our internal models of reality, so that the discontinuity is diminished. We can grow through the process of self-discovery (where we shall usually need coaching and support) so that, as our thinking adjusts, the *possibility* of the change emerges, then the *probability*, and finally the change becomes *expected*.

There are few exceptions, and these tend to be when we are not in a normal state. For instance, I have been told that if someone is becoming hysterical, a quick, sudden slap can stop deterioration and bring the individual back to normality. This makes a lot of sense if we accept that sudden, unanticipated change that is unconnected causes a form of reversal thinking, like disbelief. If we reverse an abnormality, we get normality.

One of the reasons why the Japanese have been so successful is that change for them is a series of small, incremental, connected and continuous steps. They leave the big ideas to others—and then borrow them!

Unfortunately, many of us succumb to the *'psychology of the sudden'* in some situations, e.g. terminating a business relationship. We make up our minds in isolation and without involving the 'object' to be discarded. That's our first mistake.

This can be a slow process, and, in the meantime, the object, not being a complete idiot, picks up the vibes from the insidious grapevine—the harmful substitute for open discussion and dialogue.

The employee says: 'Boss, I've heard that there are going to be quite a few redundancies. What do you think my chances are?' 'Wildly exaggerated, George, wildly exaggerated. I don't think you are at risk.' After all, we've got to get some more work out of him before he 'leaves'!

So we are hoist by our own petard. We cannot reverse the false expectations we have set. We dilly and we dally. We get more and more uncomfortable in the presence of the soon-to-be-dearly-departed, find dissembling difficult, start to blame them (of all people!), which helps our internal psychology. Then it all boils over and it's D-Day. 'You're fired'— followed by rapid exit of the 'object'.

Sometimes, we have the fall guy to carry the bad tidings—the personnel officer!

For the poor old person at the receiving end, not only is the change sudden and unpleasant, but it is also completely unexpected—and none of this is necessary. We all have a lot to learn about managing change effectively!

Frequency

A change can be a single, discrete event or can be regularly repeated. A single drop of water on the head has marginal impact. Regular, repeated drops are referred to as 'Chinese Water Torture'. It is a maxim of many change gurus (Roger Harrison as an example) that one should only intervene to the extent required to produce the result required *and no more*. Change should never become a blunt instrument.

Duration

The actual event can last for a second or for years. A sudden event can have permanent impact, as the responses to the questionnaire in Chapter 3 will prove, and as is considered in more detail in Chapter 5, 'Reacting to change'. A change process, such as a new project or going to a new school or house or job, can last much longer from beginning to end, and have much less impact.

Initiator

This is one of the key variables. If we initiate the change, or have been consulted and involved in the decision, then we tend to be much more comfortable with the change than if it is imposed or announced as a *fait accompli*. This is probably the single most important point in the whole area of creating growth from change.

Development level

As set out in Chapter 4, 'Development levels and leadership', the development level on which we are currently operating will have a major impact on how we react to change, and whether and how successfully we initiate change. Few of us are fighting for *survival*, but some of us are trying to gain *security*. If we are, we are likely to be in control mode–to impose change in a highly regulated manner, where we cannot avoid it. Most of us are building our *self-esteem*, striving for success as defined by our value systems.

While we shall often initiate change and react positively to change (provided it is not sudden and perceived as negative, in which case we shall move into security mode), the emphasis tends to be on ourselves rather than on any others affected, and on logical implications rather than on creative exploration, which can limit the degree of resulting success.

Some of us most of the time, and most of us some of the time, will be at the *growth* level, where we have the inner confidence to focus on others affected and explore and challenge the dynamics of change itself.

Perception

How we perceive change is very important. When we are initiating change for others, we should try to manage their perceptions as a conscious and structured strategic process.

If we change the perceptions of others, we shall change their reality. Equally, if we change our perceptions, we shall change our reality. This is one of the key themes considered in subsequent chapters. A true story, which took place in an Oxford college in the 1930s, proves the point.

CASE STUDY   There were a group of high-spirited undergraduates who took a dislike to another undergraduate, who was a rather weak and anaemic character. They decided to play a prank on him, and to make the prank as real as possible. They were fairly inebriated when they carried it out.

They kidnapped their victim, took him underground to a dank cellar, and told him that he was going to die—all delivered very solemnly. To give credence to their threat, they pointed to a block of wood and a sharp axe they had put there earlier. They wore down his disbelief and prepared to deliver the final act.

They bound him, gagged him and blindfolded him. In a fully ritualistic way, they led him to the block and laid his head on it. One of the group raised the axe to deliver the blow, and, at just the appropriate moment, another drew a wet towel quickly across his neck.

The undergraduate died.

Perception is reality.

Expectation

Expectations and their management are key to gaining growth. How we can optimize this variable is set out in Chapter 7. Perception, expectation, continuity and phasing are closely linked variables. Change that is suddenly presented will represent a discontinuity, if the event is unexpected—such as the sack for some.

However, an event can happen suddenly, and although the timing may be unexpected the event may not be, in which case it will not represent a discontinuity. An example would be an elderly relative who is slowly dying and suddenly passes away three months earlier than expected.

If we explicitly manage expectations, we change perceptions; but how we are perceived by others may not match what we expect. How often have we made a small intervention—perhaps some constructive advice (our perception)—and had our heads bitten off as a result, much to our surprise and subsequent annoyance. The individual concerned perceived our intervention radically different. The question of gaps in behavioural intention, manifestation and impact is covered in Chapter 7.

Impact

This variable is different in nature to the others. The others are causal variables. The variables that are operating on the various dimensions will determine the impact. The impact can be shallow or deep, temporary or permanent or, like all the other factors, somewhere in between.

When initiating change, it is essential to identify the variables and the dimensions and to consider the impact. The marvellous reality is that by a little thought and a little planning, we can alter the dimensions and hence the impact.

In effect,

WE CAN ENSURE THAT GROWTH IS CREATED

and shall return to this in more detail in Chapter 6, 'Initiating change'.

Dilemma of change

Having considered the dimensions of change, we look at the key dilemma change poses for individuals and organizations. There are two contradictory aspects of change, labelled the *uncertainty* aspect and the *unpredictability* aspect.

To make the dilemma clear, a *ceteris paribus* approach is used. This means that each aspect is examined as if it was the only one, as well as the strategic responses that are made in an attempt to resolve that aspect of change. From this perspective, it is easy to see the dilemma. What many companies and individuals do in real life is:

- pursue one set of responses to too great an extent, which limits or denies growth

- pursue both sets of responses but in such a way that there is conflict or confusion, which again limits or denies growth.

Table 1.2 presents the key responses under each aspect. Let us start with 'uncertainty'.

Table 1.2 Dilemma of change

Key aspect	Uncertainty	Unpredictability
Implication	The future *must* be determined in advance	A different future cannot be predicted
Strategic responses	■ Determining direction and purpose—mission, vision and values	■ Scenario planning—generating alternative possible futures
	■ Planning and budgeting	■ Exploration, discovery and risk-taking
	■ Objectives and targets	■ Empowerment and delegation
	■ Structure and systems	■ Building teams
	■ Cultural homogeneity	■ Cultural diversity
	■ 'Need to know' information flows	■ Sharing information
	■ 'Command and control' leadership	■ 'Empowering' leadership
Purpose	Generate certainty through control	Increase probability of successful outcomes—manage difference for value
Thinking approaches	'Left' brain ■ logical ■ systematic	'Right' brain: ■ creative ■ intuitive
Extreme position	Ossification leading to bankruptcy	Chaos leading to break-up

Uncertainty

When there is a change or a series of changes, we are faced with difference and with replacement of the known with the unknown. Where we were previously comfortable and sure of things, we are now uncomfortable and unsure of things. This leads to a certain anxiety, and if the change is perceived as negative, we can be frightened.

This can happen even with small changes—particularly with unexpected ones. So if our boss suddenly criticizes us, we may fight back and reject the criticism, or justify our behaviour, or counter-attack or accept, depending on the nature of the criticism, our relationship with our boss and our own personality. But we will often feel a frisson of fear, as it is bad news for our career if our boss thinks we are poor performers.

How can we reduce the cause of this anxiety or fear? Ignoring the extreme reactions (see Chapter 5) of total rejection or disbelief, the instinctive response to what is fundamentally an emotional reaction is to control, to create certainty, and to generate order to eliminate the burgeoning threat of chaos. Chaos is the consequence of a cumulation of differences that have no direction or purpose, i.e. are random.

And that is exactly what organizations and individuals do to remove the uncertainty created by change. Such responses, of course, are predicated on the implicit assumption that the future can be predicted or, in fact, *must* be predicted in the present.

THIS ASSUMPTION IS INVALID BUT NOT RECOGNIZED AS SUCH BECAUSE IT IS IMPLICIT

Looking at the list of organizational responses, you will notice that all these responses have occurred, and are occurring, in many companies who have experienced the changing dynamics of the 1980s—globalization, deregulation, geopolitical and economic change, demographic change, increasing buyer power and sophistication, increasing competition and new competitors, technological change, reducing entry barriers and so on—not to mention the recession, which has accentuated the intensity of this type of response as it has increased the uncertainty and fear factor.

Unpredictability

In a world of continuity and stability, the future can be predicted as if it is a continuation of the present or an extrapolation of the past. In fact, post-war there was a period of some stability and continuity and companies did just that—planned by numbers, and out rolled the profits.

Once change entered the equation, there was an increasing deviation of the actual future from the predicted future. As a result, many established companies in existing industries were unable to cope as they applied their methods from the unchanging past to the now changing future. We witnessed the demise of companies and entire industries from a purely 'British' perspective—such as cars, textiles, motor-cycles and perhaps ship-building and steel.

Unless change is small and incremental—i.e. strongly connected to the present—its consequences cannot be predicted in advance of the unravelling of those changes. The different future cannot be predicted in the present.

Now what do individuals and organizations do if they cannot predict their future business environment, and accept that they cannot (the lack of acceptance is on the other 'uncertainty' side)? They try to increase the probability of successful outcomes, creating difference and managing difference for value being a key strategy. They indulge in scenario planning, not strategic planning to a defined future goal. They encourage exploration and discovery, experiment and risk:

> 'Now I know I cannot predict the future, but I also know that it is going to be different. So we shall need lots of ideas, lots of mistakes and experiments, voyages of discovery that will lead to disaster as well as triumph. We need to create an organization that is proactive, fluid, dynamic and flexible.'

Teams are a core response, as they are an excellent mechanism for creating and managing diversity for value.

Empowerment (that much over-used word) and delegation are also part of the 'unpredictability' response. Empowerment results from recognition that those closer to the coal face will have a greater understanding of how to find and dig coal.

Delegation results from recognition that strategic thinking and change management are key responsibilities for decision takers and prerequisites in a changing world. So time has to be found to look to the future as well as manage implementation in the present.

However, these approaches, taken to extreme, lead to chaos and break-up—too many individuals or teams going in different directions.

Again, we can see that many of these responses have been used by companies in recent years as the winds of change blew into a gale. In fact the same companies have used both sets of responses with less than perfect results, usually because of a lack of understanding of how to achieve a holistic or integrated approach (discussed in Chapter 9). They have not realized that change is a key process that needs to be analysed, understood and strategically planned. It is by accident and not design. That is a key point worth noting when we are at the receiving end of changes decreed by others.

Decision takers do their level best to create success. They devote enormous energy and time to achieve this goal; they create enormous stress and strain on themselves and their families and many sacrifice their retirement. (They die in harness, or very shortly afterwards.)

A widely travelled businessman, who had worked in all areas of the world, apart from Latin America, was asked what similarities, if any, had he uncovered between the different nationalities? He said there were three:

1. Each race thought they were more different from other races than they actually were.
2. No one goes to work to do a bad job.
3. Everyone wants to improve their lot.

Many fail because they do not recognize that they need, above all, to learn how to create growth from change. Running a company successfully now is not sufficient to create success in the changing future.

Organizational learning

In a world of change and difference, one key to success is organizational learning, and that requires the leaders to lead the learning, so that they can also lead the change.

The key knowledge they need, and the skill they need to acquire, are the nature of change and how it is managed for growth.

The newly appointed CEO (chief executive officer) of a large international travel services company recognized that the culture of the company would have to change if they were going to survive. Markets were being attacked, margins were being eroded and the future looked bleak.

The existing culture contained a high level of control, regulation and procedure. The CEO discovered the Holy Grail—the one right answer: *empowerment*.

The command came down from on high: 'You are empowered'. Within a few weeks, bonfire parties were being held by joyous staff as they burned the numerous tomes containing the rules and regulations from which, with one bound, they were free. Within a few months chaos threatened, and the chastened CEO had to seize control and retire to rethink a process he did not understand. Without learning, he is unlikely to succeed.

Are you?

The dilemma can be summarized as:

INFLEXIBLE MEANS TO A DEFINED END

versus

FLEXIBLE MEANS TO AN UNCLEAR END

Balance is the key. It is true that many companies err too much on the 'uncertainty' response. This is because they already have considerable structure, system, regulation and procedure in place. So *different* structures, systems, regulations and procedures are seen as the natural way to manage the change that has produced this uncertainty.

But structure and system, direction and purpose are vital. Human beings will not operate well in a climate of chaos!

EXAMPLE   City Law firms have been blown by the winds of recession and change in the marketplace—globalization, increasing competition including new competitors like accountancy firms and in-house company lawyers, pressure on fees, more demanding and discerning clients and so on.

Some have weathered the storm better than others. Those that have done relatively well have had two things going for them—effective management structures and systems and excellent insolvency practices! Without exception, those that have done badly have had no proper management structures. These are the basics that many companies take for granted, but are the bedrock for effective change management. For instance:

■ Senior partner in the chairman role, managing partner in the chief executive officer role, supported by management and policy committees
■ Business units or departments with departmental heads and teams
■ Non-legal professionals to carry out such functional roles as personnel and marketing
■ Management information systems
■ Formal appraisal and reward systems
■ Structured training and development

and so on.

Is there a resolution to the dilemma of change? Research by the Centre of Corporate Strategy and Change, Warwick Business School, suggests that there is

FLEXIBLE MEANS TO A VISIONARY END

Learning

We learn if we understand explicitly how to learn, and apply that knowledge. In our formal education, few of us are 'taught' how to learn.

When talking about learning, I do not mean the acquisition, interpretation, analysis and evaluation of information to build know-ledge. We are, in the main, quite good at that, as that is where our formal education focuses.

No, I am talking about the application of knowledge to develop skill, which may change the way we think, our attitudes, and even our values. If we are going to do that—and that will probably be required if we are going

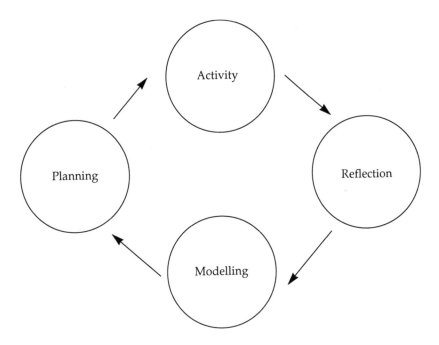

Figure 1.1 *The learning cycle.*

to get growth out of change—then we need to understand the learning process.

Let me be more specific. Let us consider first of all the learning cycle, developed by Kolb, of which there are now many variations. One version is set out in Figure 1.1.

We shall enter the cycle at *activity*—the point of entry is immaterial as the process is continuous and iterative. During an activity, we tend to be doing and feeling simultaneously. The degree to which we are likely to 'learn by doing' will depend on whether we consciously *reflect* on the activity or review the experience: what did we do or feel, and why.

Next is the need to *model*. Where does this experience and the reflection on it fit in? Have we a model or theory or framework that provides context and understanding? Can we improve and develop our model in the light of experience and reflection? We all implicitly or explicitly have mental models of reality, since reality itself is too difficult to comprehend. Making an implicit model explicit, or developing an explicit model in the light of experience and reflection, improves our learning. We make new discoveries in the process.

Finally, we need to apply our learning to a similar or new experience; we need to distil the key learning points and *plan* to improve. The application of the plan to a fresh activity completes the cycle, which, as already said, is continuous and iterative. Let us take an example:

EXAMPLE

The context is leadership and team-building, and the event about to take place is the completion of a task in an outdoor environment. There are six managers, say, and a facilitator present. One manager has been nominated to lead the exercise (no problem with acceptance of this role, as it is a leadership course and every manager will have the role for different tasks) and another to observe. He knows what to observe and why and knows that he is not allowed to speak or get involved.

Two things have occurred before this activity.

■ The modelling side of things has been covered, so that there is knowledge in the areas of leadership and teams, including knowledge of their own styles and approaches. Also, there is a process model in place—what needs to be done, why and when in order to achieve success. Plenty of theory has been covered.

■ They have had warm-up exercises, become accustomed to operating in a new environment, and are comfortable with physical contact—touching. If you are about to manoeuvre your way through a small hole of what is (nominally!) an electrified lattice of rope, and you know that if you touch any part of the rope you are 'dead' and your team has failed, you will want support—both emotional and physical. Whether you get it or not is a function of team spirit and cohesion, the development of which is part of the learning experience. (Growing the team is the subject of Chapter 8.)

The leader and observer are briefed by the facilitator as to objective and constraints, the clock starts, and 20 minutes later, it stops. The task may or may not have been completed, that is not the main issue—the key is how the task was tackled.

The leadership model and process model are examined in the light of experience. What did the leader do and how was it done? Was information shared, and did everyone understand the objective? How were ideas generated and developed? What roles were allocated, why, and when? How was the technical aspect dealt with? Who was 'in the helicopter' ensuring that mistakes were not carelessly made and that individuals were not idle or in conflict or feeling isolated? Was the leader controlling or coordinating—and so on?

The review and feedback do not take much time, because there is an overall context. Next, can we refine the models so that they are relevant to this group, with its special skills and talents? What are the key learning points to be distilled for the next exercise? What is the plan to improve, and apply to the next task?

Without exception, a day of similar and different activities that follow the learning cycle lead to effective learning. Usually, at the end, there are powerful self-managing teams who do not need a facilitator. There is strong mutual support and an open atmosphere of dialogue and debate where feelings can be expressed, and where the understanding of the nature and reality of effective leadership has fundamentally altered from the initial mind-set.

Before looking at the relevance of the learning cycle to change (the subject-matter of this book), I would like to introduce another aspect of learning: the learning ladder (Figure 1.2). The base level—level 0—is where we do not perceive the need to learn. If we are not aware that we don't know, then we cannot learn. This is called unconscious incompetence! If you do not consciously perceive any need to get growth out of change, then you won't.

The next level is where we recognize that we have something to learn—we know that we don't know (everything). Level 1 is referred to as conscious incompetence. The move from Level 0 to Level 1 usually causes discomfort, because we are admitting to ourselves that we do not know.

This should be balanced by the fact that we actually know more than we now think, as we are about to discover. The next level is where, through the development and application of knowledge (by implementing the learning cycle) we begin to 'know that we know'—we become consciously competent.

Practice improves, though never makes perfect. The result of practice over time is Level 3, the highest level, where we 'don't know we know' or are unconsciously competent.

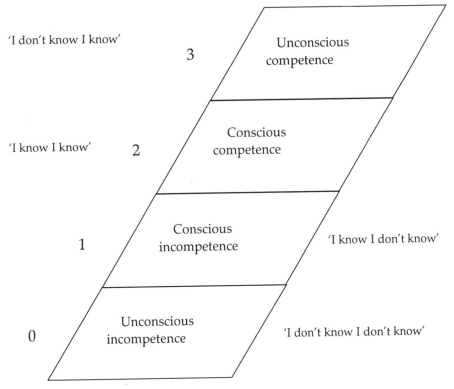

Figure 1.2 *The learning ladder.*

EXAMPLE A very good example of this is driving a car. When we are very young, we do not know we need to learn to drive, and we do not want to learn. Because of the symbolism of the car, and the importance to modern day life, most of us, when young children, move to Level 1. We know that we cannot drive and want to learn, and what is more we can't until the advanced age of 17—very frustrating.

Then we start taking driving lessons, and pass our test and, for many, we stay at Level 1 for some time! It needs quite a lot of time and the application of knowledge in the practical context of actually driving for us to move to Level 2— where we are consciously competent in our driving.

Over time two things happen. We move up to Level 3 and down to Level 0! Driving becomes habitual: the learning is internalized. So we can drive well without conscious thought. How many of us on a familiar route have suddenly realized that we have driven the last few miles without any conscious effort?

We have unconscious competence, but unconscious incompetence! We have developed bad habits, which we don't consciously recognize in ourselves, though we seem to have a highly developed sense of their presence in others!

There is one learning from this reality–the need to consciously revisit the learning ladder and cycle, even when we think we have learned! It's not easy.

CASE STUDY   Different models have a different impact on different people. The learning ladder usually has some impact on all of us, but the greatest impact, from experience, is on lawyers.

Sundridge Park uses a Performance Improvement Process, whereby delegates on a programme rate their knowledge or skill in the key topic areas before the programme, at the end, and three months afterwards. A manager rates the delegates for the first and last periods.

Usually, the self-assessment goes up significantly at the end of the programme (thank God) and is maintained overall with some falling back in some areas, but with further development in others to compensate. The manager tends to agree with the 'subordinate', although there can be specific gaps in perception which need to be addressed.

One group of partners from a City Law firm were very taken by the learning ladder. At the end of the programme, they all marked themselves down! As they said: 'Before attending the programme, we marked ourselves highly in all the areas. Now we realize that we knew much less than we thought we did, and although we have learned a lot (especially from each other), we realize that we have a lot more to learn!'

So what? What, you ask, is the relevance of this to getting personal growth out of change?

Well, I hope you travel through both the learning cycle and the learning ladder as you read this book. I have already introduced some models and some experience, but there are necessarily others. At the end of this and every chapter, I shall summarize what I think are the key learning points. I shall also leave space for you to make your notes, as learning is unique to each individual.

While it is important to recognize strengths (which can often be latent) to build confidence, it is also important to recognize areas where you need to learn—to move from Level 0 to Level 1 on the learning ladder. I hope, at this early stage, there has been enough stimulation in the material for you to feel that there are areas in which you can improve.

In the subsequent chapters, I ask you to discover more about yourself and how you approach change, to reflect on a change experience that has had a major impact in the past and distil your own learning points. I also set out how you can improve in such relevant areas as promoting discovery, managing expectations and developing consistency between behavioural intent, manifestation and impact.

I provide opportunities for you to close the learning loop through action planning. As I said in the Preface, this book has been designed as a learning vehicle as well as a guide.

This brings me to the final section of this first chapter: action planning. I appreciate that many of you will be familiar with this, but a practical example that brings out the need to set measurable objectives and milestones will perhaps be a useful refresher.

Action planning

The starting point is the desire to improve in an area where personal value will be gained if we succeed, and where we recognize that there is room for improvement. We need to be personally motivated. Without that, any action plan will stay in the mind or on paper.

Next we have to know when we have succeeded. We have to set ourselves an overall objective, bound by time and measurable, whether quantitatively or qualitatively. Then we must determine the steps we need to take, and in what time-frame, to achieve our objective. You may also need interim milestones on the way to reaching the objective.

I take *listening* as the area in which we have decided to improve. This is a good area in the context of gaining growth from change, as good listening skills are essential to pick up spoken and non-spoken messages from the initiators of change, and help in persuading others to change, in promoting discovery, managing expectations and so on.

The action plan is by way of example. If *you* were to choose listening as one of the areas you wanted to work on, the plan would be *your* plan, not mine, and would be different.

The plan

Objective (three months)

- I shall ask three people I know (whom I shall select randomly at the time from a shortlist of 10 that I shall now draw up) whether they think I have become a better listener. They will all say 'yes' and, when asked to estimate the degree of change, state that my degree of improvement is at least 50 per cent compared with my listening ability three months previously.

Milestones

- 2 months: Consciously and actively listening 10 times a day.
- 6 weeks: Consciously and actively listening 5 times a day.

Actions

- End week 1: Completed research and obtained information and equipment—bought good book on body language and listening, obtained access to video equipment and camcorder.
- End week 2: Read books and noted key points.
- End week 3: Drew up action plan.
- End week 4: Carried out exercises with trusted friend, studied video and noted how to listen effectively.
- End week 5: Started conscious active listening, recording my feelings and how the other party reacted.

And so on.

Key point summary

Dimensions of change

- Change can be characterized by different variables, each with its own dimension.
- If the *environment* is one of change, a negative attitude from employees can arise due to too much control, regulation, structure and procedure *and* a perceived excess of changes.

- Encouraging creativity and involvement leads to a more positive response.

- Asking the right questions in an environment of change is important. For example, the logical 'What do we need to do differently to respond to change?' is easier to answer and less critical than the question 'How do we ensure that we obtain agreement to what needs to be done and it is carried through?'

- Change means changing attitudes to risk; being prepared to take more risk than was necessary in times of stability.

- *Discontinuity* leads to discomfort and resistance.

- Initiators of change should seek to build the best of the old into the new and stress continuity and connection, when 'selling' change.

- Those taking on new roles should adopt the 100-day rule before implementing change: listen and learn for the first 100 days.

- Where, however, there is organizational or individual inertia, a jolt to the system needs to be provided.

- The more *significant* and *sudden* a change is, the more resistance there will be. Significant change should be broken down into smaller components and phased in gradually.

- Due to the 'psychology of the sudden', business relationships can be terminated in an unnecessarily harsh and ineffective manner. Strategies should be developed to avoid this.

- Change should not be a blunt instrument. The *frequency* of intervention should be limited to producing the result required.

- Managing our perceptions and expectations and those of others is critical for gaining growth from change.

- We can improve the impact of change by altering the dimensions of the variables *before* implementation. Change itself should be strategically planned.

Dilemma of change

- Change poses a fundamental dilemma. The response to 'uncertainty' is to define the future *which cannot be defined*, control the present and follow a disciplined and structured path to the defined future. The response to 'unpredictability' is empowering others, generating ideas, taking risks, creating teams—encouraging a culture of diversity, exploration and flexibility.

- There are *inflexible means to a defined end* or *flexible means to an unclear end*.

- The two approaches are incompatible. Individuals and organizations can follow one approach to too great an extent or have an unplanned and unhappy mix over time.

- Balancing the two—resolving the dilemma—is a key strategic necessity if growth is to be obtained from change. Research suggests that the best mix is 'flexible means to a visionary end'.

Learning

- Learning involves applying the learning cycle: activity, reflection, modelling and planning for the next experience.

- Learning also involves climbing the learning ladder: moving from unconscious incompetence through to unconscious competence. Applying the learning cycle moves the individual from unconscious incompetence to conscious competence.

- Action planning is required to close the cycle—to translate theory into practice. Motivation to improve in the chosen area is a key prerequisite. An objective, measurable and defined by time, must be set, with interim milestones. Actions bound by deadlines and sequenced complete the plan.

Your own points

Discovery

Introduction

Having considered the dimensions and dilemma of change, looked at learning and summarized the key points, I now ask you to look at yourselves. By this I mean start a process of conscious recognition of your individual approach to change: think of your preferences and of how they combine to produce your profile, and consider what it all means.

This is achieved by a simple self-assessment shown on the following pages. When you have completed this, there is a guide to the scoring, the end product of which is your profile, set out in the form of a bar chart. This gives an easy visual demonstration of the particular approach you prefer, and the one you like least.

Having explained what it all means, I consider the profiles of six people (real people with names changed) for three reasons:

1. We can learn a little through looking at others.

2. The analysis will help you interpret your own profile better.

3. You may have a very similar profile.

I would mention that *you decide* whether the answers have relevance and are helpful. There is no magic or mystery in assessments. They simply reflect what you say about yourself. They neither do nor should attempt the impossible: putting a human being into a box or boxes. Their value is that they enable us:

■ to reflect upon what we may know, but which is usually at the level of unconscious competence; if we are going to learn a little bit more, we need to bring our self-knowledge back down to conscious competence;

■ to put that knowledge into a context or model, which we may not have had before; this too can improve our learning by building the 'big picture' and showing where we fit in.

So, please read the next section carefully, complete and score the change preference assessment, and produce your profile.

Change preference assessment

For each of the areas covered, please choose the phrase, word, action and so on with which you identify the most. Give that preference 4 marks. In each category, there are four choices, and so you need to allocate 3 marks to your next choice, then 2, and finally 1 mark for the item with which you least identify.

Let us take the first example, where you imagine that you have total freedom to choose any of four different jobs, as set out below. In this case, I have chosen administrator (4 marks), followed by researcher (3 marks), followed by writer (2 marks), with social worker bringing up the rear with the final single point.

1. *Jobs*   *Marks*

   Researcher

   Administrator

   Writer

   Social worker

A	3
B	4
C	2
D	1

Please complete the form, and record your score on the score chart on page 27. The mark for each set of choices should be transferred to one of four categories LD, NC, PF, PC, appropriately labelled: e.g. the score for C in question 1 will be placed in the PC column.

1. *Jobs*   *Marks*

   Researcher

   Administrator

   Writer

   Social worker

A	
B	
C	
D	

2. *Words*

   Harmony

   Beauty

   Intellect

   Efficiency

A	
B	
C	
D	

3. *Words*
    Keep
    Evaluate
    Share
    Change

	Marks
A	
B	
C	
D	

4. *Words*
    Idea
    Feeling
    Organization
    Fact

A	
B	
C	
D	

5. *Phrases*
    The right answer
    Safety first
    Go for it
    Sixth sense

A	
B	
C	
D	

6. *Sayings*
    Smile and the whole world smiles with you
    Nothing ventured, nothing gained
    The facts speak for themselves
    Look before you leap

A	
B	
C	
D	

7. *How someone who did not like you might describe you*
    Being stuck in the mud
    Being as dry as dust
    Wearing your heart on your sleeve
    Having your head in the clouds

A	
B	
C	
D	

8. *Attitude to risk: do you prefer to*   *Marks*

Take risks?

A	
B	
C	
D	

Share risks?

Avoid risks?

Analyse risks?

9. *Attitude to change: do you prefer to*

Analyse and evaluate ideas?

A	
B	
C	
D	

Implement ideas that are practical?

Generate ideas?

Look to see how ideas will affect others?

10. *Actions you take: do you prefer to*

Make a new friend?

A	
B	
C	
D	

Change your approach?

Have a debate?

Control a situation?

11. *How you would describe yourself?*

Practical

A	
B	
C	
D	

Rational

Friendly

Imaginative

12. *How someone who did not like you might describe you*

Rebellious

A	
B	
C	
D	

Weak

Over-cautious

Cold

Now record your scores on the chart on page 27 and enter your profile in the manner shown in the example.

SCORE CHART

Question Number	LD		NC		PF		PC	
1.	A	4	B	3	D	2	C	1
2.	C	2	D	3	A	4	B	1
3.	B	2	A	3	C	1	D	4
4.	D	2	C	1	B	3	A	4
5.	A	1	B	3	D	4	C	2
6.	C	1	D	2	A	4	B	3
7.	B	1	A	3	C	4	D	2
8.	D	2	C	1	B	3	A	4
9.	A	4	B	3	D	2	C	1
10.	C	2	D	3	A	1	B	4
11.	B	1	A	4	C	3	D	2
12.	D	3	C	2	B	1	A	4

TOTALS   25 + 31 + 30 + 32 = 120   118

YOUR PROFILE

Preference	LD	NC	PF	PC
High 48 — 36				
Moderate 24		1	t	
Low 12				
SCORE				

EXAMPLE

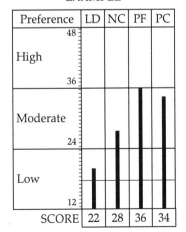

Preference	LD	NC	PF	PC
High 48 — 36				
Moderate 24				
Low 12				
SCORE	22	28	36	34

Origin

Before interpreting the profile, I should satisfy the natural curiosity that many of you will have as to the origins of the questionnaire. This need was heightened for me, because two expert reviewers of an earlier version of this book thought they had uncovered a truth that I had deliberately concealed. One was convinced that 'the one right answer' was Freud, and the other that 'the one right answer' was Myers Briggs. Both were wrong.

I devised the actual questionnaire, the focus on change, and the labels. The model that I used, which focuses on cognitive learning and the thinking/feeling processes of the brain (and is not concerned specifically with approaches to change) is Ned Hermann's. I would refer you to his excellent work *The Creative Brain* for full details. He has devised a detailed questionnaire that identifies which of the four possible 'quadrants of the brain' an individual prefers to use, can use or avoids using and what that means in terms of behaviour and relationships.

With gross simplification and apologies to Mr Hermann, some of you may be familiar with the division of the brain into 'left' and 'right'.

- *Left brain approach*: fact-based, analytical, step-by-step, favouring words, numbers and facts, presented in logical sequence.

- *Right brain approach*: seek out insights, images, patterns, sounds and movement, all to be synthesized into an intuitive sense of the whole.

What Ned Hermann has done, with years of research to prove his conclusions, is to add another dimension to produce four quadrants, separating the brain horizontally between the 'cerebral' or intellectual and 'limbic' or emotional.

I have taken the four processing modes as the base for an examination of attitudes to change. One could ignore all the background and simply say, from a common sense point of view (in fact my starting point, until I had to consider retrospectively what had formed the base of that common sense):

- we can be emotionally *detached*, accept, think *logically* about the implications of change, or

- we can be emotionally involved, *negative* about change and try to limit the damage or *control* the impact of change, or

- we can accept and *focus* on the impact on other *people* involved, or

- we can be intellectually stimulated, be *creative* and *positively* explore and change the dynamics of change.

Interpretation

Please look at Figures 2.1 to 2.6, which explain what the initials stand for, and set out some of the activities, attitudes and approaches associated with each preference or *mode*.

The first point to make is that, apart from one or two exceptional people, we operate in different modes at different times when experiencing change. However, we may have a strong preference for a particular mode, in which case we are likely to rely on that approach most of the time.

Before interpreting the profile as a whole, let us first look at each mode, as if we were operating in that mode, and consider what that means in terms of approach.

Logical Detached (LD)

In this mode, we are unemotional, and have a rational perspective. We shall be interested in the facts of the matter, and the implications—trying to make sense of things. We won't be challenging the nature and dimensions of the change, nor considering the emotional impact on ourselves or others, but focusing on an analysis of the event and what it means.

Analyse and evaluate	Explore and discover
Resist and stay in control	Accept and help others

Figure 2.1 *The four change preferences.*

INTERNAL FOCUS	EXTERNAL FOCUS	
LD Logical Detached	PC Positive Creative	INTELLECTUAL
Negative Control NC	People Focused PF	EMOTIONAL
LEFT BRAIN	RIGHT BRAIN	

Figure 2.2 *The divisions of the brain.*

EXAMPLE Let us take an example. We shall use the same example in each case, so that the differences can be highlighted. Let us assume that we have been told by the personnel department that there may be a promotion for us from, say, assistant manager in our section to manager.

As logical detached people, the promotion makes obvious sense in career progression terms. We would find out such things as when the promotion was to occur, why we had been selected, what it meant in extra pay and non-financial benefits; we would check up that our understanding of the role and responsibilities was clear, whether there were any rivals for the job, what the selection process and timing would be, what the probability of getting the job would be, and so on—all the logical questions.

If the answers made sense, we would be happy. The LD approach is closed in the sense that we accept the change for what it is, and then ask the questions that resolve the issues arising from the change.

In real life, we would not stay in that mode throughout, particularly when we first learned about the change. If we have a very high LD score, and there is a big gap between that and the next score, the chances are we are very logical, emotionally controlled people, and would react in the way suggested.

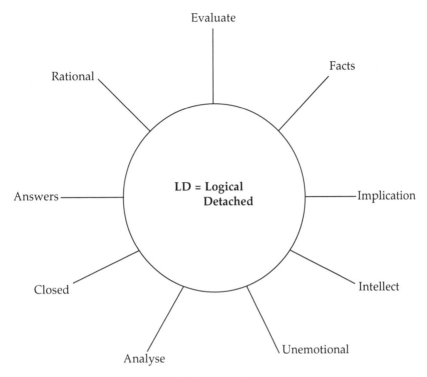

Figure 2.3 *The Logical Detached approach to change.*

Negative Control (NC)

In this mode our reaction is fundamentally emotional, negative and self-centred. We shall instinctively resist the change, because it necessarily disrupts the status quo, with which we are happy. Depending on the nature of the change (and this aspect is covered in detail in Chapter 5, 'Reacting to change'), we may deny its existence, as can happen with sudden and traumatic changes.

We are in a fight to control our environment, under threat from the change. We shall automatically tend to accentuate the negative, expressing our views logically and, if necessary, illogically. If we fight in vain, and the change is forced upon us, then we shall try to minimize the damage and maximize the connection to the present and past.

So when we hear about the possible promotion, our instant internal reaction is 'No thanks!'. Politically, that might not be possible to state baldly, and so we might demur, mentioning how happy we are in the current role, and how good we are at that job, or we might try to postpone, suggesting the timing is not quite

EXAMPLE

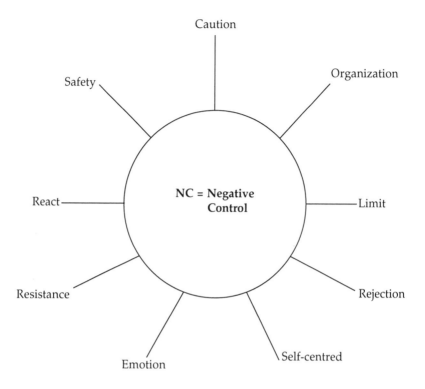

Figure 2.4   *The Negative Control approach to change.*

right—a year or so later, we would absolutely love promotion, or we might go the 'I don't feel I am quite ready for it, haven't developed the right skills yet' supplementary approach.

However, if our fight is in vain, and we are promoted, then we shall have a pragmatic and organized approach so that the new environment can become comfortable as soon as possible.

People Focused (PF)

In this mode, we tend to accept the change, rather than challenge, explore or resist the experience; we react emotionally rather than intellectually, and our primary focus is not ourselves but others, who are affected by the change. Our emotional needs are likely to be satisfied by sharing the experience as far as possible—thereby gaining support—and providing support to those also affected.

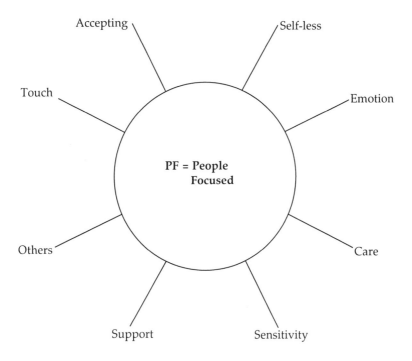

Figure 2.5 *The People Focused approach to change.*

Taking the example of the possible promotion, we are likely to be pleased, want **EXAMPLE** to share the good news with colleagues, friends and relatives. We shall be concerned with the impact it will have on all the staff in the section, how they will react to our more senior status in the same department, particularly former peers, who will be put in a subordinate role to us.

Positive Creative (PC)

In this mode, we enjoy change, like taking risks, and want to be part of the future that change is creating. We tend not to be emotionally involved with the consequences of change on ourselves and others but are wrapped up in the dynamics of change—full of questions and ideas as we explore the possibilities change brings in its wake.

Considering the possible promotion, we would be interested in making sure we **EXAMPLE** knew what the job entailed, we would be enthusiastic, we would explore the boundaries and constraints, challenge them, consider new approaches (as, in this instance, we would have a good idea of the current job, as it is held by our boss), new ways of meeting the objectives and new objectives to meet.

In real life, if we only used this mode, we probably would not get the job! The

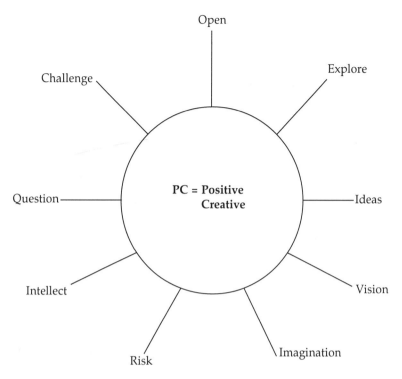

Figure 2.6   *The Positive Creative approach to change.*

likely reaction of a boss (to whom inevitably we would be talking at some stage), whose job is being given to a subordinate who questions and challenges that boss's approach (which is likely to be the perception of the boss, though not the intention of the subordinate with his or her PC hat on) would be negative.

The profile

The assessment forced us to choose, and so the profile indicates which mode or modes we prefer. The stronger the preference in relative terms, the more likely are we to adopt the particular mode or modes preferred, when experiencing change.

Additionally, *the profile indicates the extent to which we are likely to initiate change*. For instance, if we have a score of, say, 36 or more in PC (Positive Creative) and 24 or less in NC (Negative Control), showing that PC is a strong mode and NC is a weak mode, then we shall often be initiators of change, whereas with the reverse scoring we shall be maintainers of the status quo.

As mentioned at the beginning of this chapter, I propose–as I do not know your scores–to consider six profiles of other people's scores and highlight the key implications. This, I think, will help your understanding of the implications behind your own profile.

Let us turn to the six profiles (all names have been changed).

Hazel

LD	NC	PF	PC
22	30	**38**	30

I have emboldened the strongest preference and italicized the weakest, which will be a consistent approach throughout.

Hazel's preferred mode is People Focused (PF), with Positive Creative (PC) and Negative Control (NC) in support or secondary. The gap of 8 between PF and PC/NC is significant. The Logical Detached (LD) approach is only occasionally used.

Hazel appears fundamentally caring for others and concerned with how others will be affected by change–emotionally involved, rather than intellectually involved. The combined 'emotional' scores (NC + PF; 30 + 38 = 68) are significantly higher than the combined intellectual scores (LD + PC; 22 + 30 = 52).

Within the emotional side, the desire to be in control and to be safe is quite strong. This could lead to tension when Hazel's feelings for others and the exciting creative side conflicts with the need to stay in control, keep both feet on the ground and connect back to the present and the past.

Within the intellectual side, there is a preference towards the possibilities of change, and excitement with change itself rather than a detached analysis of the consequences of change.

Change for Hazel which would be most acceptable would need to:

- be exciting

- be connected to the past

- ensure that she stays in control

- occur with another person.

Hazel would find it tough to change circumstances without support. The high PF score does indicate that Hazel could be bullied into change by a strong personality, with whom she is emotionally involved.

As regards initiating change, the difference between her PC and NC scores is exactly zero, and, in the absence of the involvement of another person (a shared venture), she is unlikely to be very proactive.

Note: As I said before, the results are as valid as you perceive them.

However, although I do not know many of the respondents to the assessment, I do know some. With some of those, I have discussed the interpretation. To date, there has been a consensus as to meaning.

Rodney

LD	NC	PF	PC
30	*15*	**37**	**38**

A difference of one or two points between scores is not significant. We see that Rodney has two preferred modes—People Focused and Positive Creative with Logical Detached in support. There is a very low Negative Control score (the minimum possible is 12).

Rodney is an individual who likes change and will often initiate it (the difference between the PC and NC scores is a very large 24), and is happy to involve others or at least one other (high PF). There is a strong intellectual bias ($68 - 52 = 16$) combining both the creative and evaluative aspects (LD = 30).

With the very low NC score, he would be able to react well to traumatic events, by being able to give and receive emotional support, through rationalization and through the strong PC aspect. He would be able to look beyond and around the event, and generate options and approaches outside the limitations and perceived realities, which would bind someone with a high NC score.

However, another aspect of the low NC score is that there may well be occasions when Rodney is controlled by rather than controlling change. The low perceived preference for control can result in the absence of control.

Mabel

LD	NC	PF	PC
35	**37**	*24*	*24*

Mabel's preferred modes are Logical Detached and Negative Control, with a significant gap between those modes and the less used People Focused and Positive Creative. Mabel doesn't like change, tries to control her environment and resists change. She rarely initiates change and is not inclined to be very supportive of others experiencing change.

When change does occur, she will try to rationalize it (LD = 35) rather than challenge or modify it, and focus on producing order from the temporary chaos created. There is a certain brittleness in this profile with the emphasis on the self, the past, and detached logical thought.

Change that would be most acceptable to Mabel would need to be gradual, strongly connected to the present and the past, and where she felt in control throughout and could understand and accept the logic of it all.

Unlike Rodney, Mabel would find traumatic change particularly difficult to handle. This is, in fact, because she suffered traumatic change in the past, which has had a significant and, to date, permanent impact on her approach to change. This reality is explored in Chapter 5, where we consider some of the responses to the questionnaire, exploring a significant event or events in the past. Chapter 3 ('Reflection') considers situations of a business nature and Chapter 5 ('Reacting to change') those of a personal nature.

Author

LD	NC	PF	PC
25	18	34	**43**

There is always an issue for an author. Where should he or she be placed on the scale that runs from total ego-focus to total anonymity. If I fill this book with me, no one will read it—quite rightly. Equally, if I ask you to look at yourself and think about change and not share some of my experience, that would also be wrong. I think some self-exposure is useful, but I shall be very sparing.

My self-assessment produced the above. As you can see, the dominant mode is Positive Creative (PC) with People Focused (PF) in support, some Logical Detached (LD) and not much Negative Control (NC). Every profile has strengths and weaknesses, and mine is no exception. What is useful, a point I shall develop at the end of the chapter, is learning from the profile— and that's the toughest thing.

The danger in my profile is too much change, taking too many risks— change that is not fully thought through and has negative consequences as a result, and generating the perception by my employers that I have slightly rebellious tendencies and do not conform enough to the NC of the culture. I shall share one experience that brought some of these negative aspects home to me, but only after I had completed the assessment and realized the implication.

My secretary has a fine singing voice, and usually sings a solo at the Christmas party. She was rehearsing, just after she had received the music, and, on the spur of the moment, I sang along. Some bright spark suggested we did a duet. My secretary was delighted to share the risk. She was also concerned that the music was written in too high a key for her voice. So I volunteered to rewrite the song, and play it. I'm no pianist—I can play a basic song, after a lot of practice.

So, a few days later, in front of all the staff, I was playing the piano—the first time, I had ever done so in public. I was singing a duet, which I had never done before, and I was doing both at the same time!

EXAMPLE

I will never forget watching my left hand shaking so uncontrollably that it was almost impossible to hit the key-board. It was not a total disaster, but not far off.

That was the result of the combination of a very high PC, coupled with a fairly high PF.

Joanne

LD	NC	PF	PC
19	31	**36**	**34**

Joanne has People Focused and Positive Creative as preferred modes, with Negative Control in strong support, and very little preference for Logical Detached.

All the scores apart from LD are in the moderate range, though at the top end. There is an emotional bias (67 compared with 53) and a preference for exploring rather than evaluating change. The moderate NC score, only 5 less than PF, implies that she would tend to initiate change, which was not too radical: evolutionary rather than revolutionary.

The low LD score suggests that she does not think through the impact and implications of change, and could be caught out by unanticipated consequences. The PF score indicates support for others also involved in change, and a desire to share the experience.

Reaction to traumatic change would be quite testing (NC = 31) but helped by the PF and PC strengths.

Karl

LD	NC	PF	PC
32	*26*	30	**32**

All Karl's scores are in the moderate range, and the gap between the highest and lowest is only 6.

There is a slight intellectual bias (64 compared to 56) and a moderate difference between PC and NC of 6. Karl, like Joanne, will tend to initiate change of an evolutionary nature, rather than risky or revolutionary change. Unlike Joanne, when experiencing the change, he is likely to evaluate the impact and implications, as well as explore the possibilities and challenge the boundaries.

However, as implied by the scores, Karl is unlikely to push or challenge too far or to need a lot of control, and will only provide moderate support to others involved.

How do we compare?

While it is helpful to look at the absolute scores and the implications of differences and less or more preferred modes, additional value can be gained by comparing us with the norms—combining and averaging the scores of all those who have filled in the assessment.

There are two such profiles, as men and women are not identical, on average, for this particular assessment.

Before looking at these, I would enter a caveat about preferences. We do not always do what we would like to do. There are many factors that can create a gap between desired and actual approaches to change. Four key factors are

1. The nature of a given task or project

2. The level of stress

3. The individual relationship and the level, e.g. 'boss' or 'subordinate'

4. Aspiration without actuality.

A preference does not indicate competence or skill. In some situations, we may intend to behave in a certain way, but the behaviour we manifest may not match intention exactly, and equally the impact on someone else may be different from what we intended. This is covered in more detail in Chapter 7, 'Developing skills'.

The female profile

LD	NC	PF	PC
25	29	**37**	29

We see here NC and PC scores, which are balanced, a strong preference for PF, and an LD score at the low end of the moderate range. There is a significant preference for emotional (PF + NC = 66) rather than intellectual responses (LD + PC = 54), a difference of 12. The balance of NC and PC suggests, on average, that change initiated will be small and connected, rather than discontinuous, with a preference for a partner.

The male profile

	LD	NC	PF	PC
	27	24	33	**36**
Female	25	29	37	29
	2	(5)	(4)	7

There is a slightly greater preference for a logically detached approach, significantly less resistance, less concern with the impact on others, and considerably greater desire for positive exploration.

There is a reversal of the intellectual/emotional balance, with LD + PC = 63 and PF + PC = 57—a difference of 6.

The gap of 12 between PC and NC suggests that men are much more the initiators of change than women.

Note: This is, of course, on average. There will be many profiles of individuals that show particular orientations and preferences and have absolutely no gender bias.

Playing to strengths

There is always a danger that we start feeling dissatisfied with ourselves when we start 'objectively' considering how we approach change or the conclusions of any assessment or questionnaire. This is assuming that we don't react to any feeling of emerging conscious incompetence with the NC response: 'What a load of rubbish. I reject all this nonsense and regret wasting my hard-earned money on this book.'

In fact, the higher your NC score, the more likely that you have or are moving into a rejection mode. If you have a high LD score, you may well be finding flaws in the instrument, where you perceive a logical inconsistency, and starting the rejection process, i.e. there may be rejection on both logical and emotional grounds.

In fact, those who have a high LD/NC combination may well not be reading this section at all! This is a pity, because there is neither a right nor wrong answer nor a right nor wrong change preference mode.

A key to creating growth from change (as mentioned in the first chapter) is to develop an integrated approach using all the responses, as each is needed at different times and phases. This is particularly difficult when we are reacting to change and is much easier when we initiate change. This theme is developed in subsequent chapters.

I want to conclude this chapter by highlighting the strengths of each approach.

Logical Detached (LD)

The ability to stand back, be objective and analyse and evaluate the implications of change is essential to gaining growth. Imposing the necessary discipline of facts and information, and curbing the excess of the improbable, are vital components.

Negative Control (NC)

The language I have used is 'negative' and so the label may be a little disconcerting. I thought about labels very carefully, and am conscious that my own profile is low on NC. We often are not bothered about negative labels that do not apply to us! However, I am focusing on change, and a negative attitude is one key aspect of this mode. So I have kept it.

There are considerable strengths in this preference. We have seen that change is more acceptable, generally, if it is delivered in stages and is strongly connected to the past. In fact, the Japanese, who are a very conservative nation, have used this preference very well in developing continuous improvement cultures, where there is not change as such in the short-term but incremental improvement, based solidly on the present and past.

Paradoxically, we could argue that the NC preference is culturally too low, and is vital in obtaining continuous improvement cultures.

Provided the strong NC individual recognizes the need for improvement rather than change, he or she will be very useful in both making and selling the connections to the status quo.

People Focused (PF)

Change almost invariably involves others as well as ourselves. The ability to recognize how others are affected, to listen to and understand their concerns and to support them through change smooths the path for all of us.

Positive Creative (PC)

Change is never set in concrete. A creative, exploring and challenging approach to change can significantly improve both its nature and the outcomes for the better.

Key point summary

- Four approaches to change are examined by means of a simple self-assessment.

- In *Logical Detached* (LD) mode, we are emotionally uninvolved, accept the change, and analyse and evaluate its implications.

- In *Negative Control* (NC) mode, we tend to reject or resist change, control its impact, and connect strongly to the past.

- In *People Focused* (PF) mode, we tend to accept the change, be emotionally involved, and focus on giving support to others affected.

- In *Positive Creative* (PC) mode, we are positive towards change, and like to explore, challenge and alter the dynamics of change.

- The combination of scores provides our change preference profile, where we may prefer one approach over another.

- The greater the gap between the PC mode and the NC mode, the more likely are we to be initiators of change. If our NC score is higher than our PC score, we are likely to be maintainers of the status quo.

- Men tend to prefer a more logical approach, are less negative, provide less support and are more likely to initiate change than women.

- Gaining effective growth from change requires all approaches to be deployed at different times in the cycle.

- We should recognize the strengths in each approach, and the strengths in each of our profiles.

- The NC approach may well be undervalued. Provided there is the ability to accept the need for improvement rather than change, an NC approach is the key to developing a continuous improvement culture, and deriving the value from the past, which should be retained in the future.

Your own points

Reflection

Introduction

In this chapter I ask you to fill in a questionnaire, examining an experience of change that had an impact on your thinking, feeling and behaviour. Specific questions are set out, including what you now feel you have learned from the experience.

As one respondent said, 'I found completing this emotionally powerful—and it did highlight for me how we repeat processes in situations totally different to that which inspired the internal model.'

If we are to gain an understanding of why we approach change the way we do, we need to look back, reflect and learn—continue the process of explicit, conscious recognition.

As mentioned in the first chapter, learning from experience is one of the more powerful forms of learning, provided that we take time out to understand and reflect. As in the previous chapter, I also share with you the replies of five people who have completed the questionnaire, and link into their current profiles. In this chapter, we shall consider only events in a business context; in Chapter 5 we shall look at some replies that deal with more personal events.

I know that some people found it difficult to go through the process of looking back and reflecting, as sometimes there is a lot of pain in our past which we are reluctant to revisit. No one, as far as I am aware, has regretted completing the questionnaire—including the women who selected rape as their experience of change.

Now please complete the questionnaire below.

Your experience of change

Think of a 'change situation'—something that happened that affected your thinking, feeling and behaviour. It can be from childhood or adulthood, from personal or business life. It just needs to be an example that had, and may still be having, an impact. It could be anything—sudden or gradual.

From the sudden aspect, the range could vary from (in personal life) the sudden death of a relative to an unexpected windfall such as an inheritance or money prize, and (in business life) from being summoned for an unexpected promotion to getting the sack!

Then there is the range of changes that are more gradual in terms of learning about them and dealing with them: the possibility of parents moving house/job and you with them to a new school, or the possibility of promotion, which subsequently materializes, and so on.

It could be something purely from within, a feeling growing inside that you wanted to make a significant change in your life–leaving parents/ partner/job or whatever.

Please decide on a specific situation and then answer the questions listed.

The event

Please describe the actual event that you have selected.

Prior to the event

Q1. Assuming the actual event did not take place immediately, how did you come to realize the possibility was there?

Q2. Who was or were the sources of information, and what was your immediate emotional response? Did you feel angry or annoyed or upset or shocked or elated or excited, or whatever?

Q3. Did you have a clear picture early on of what the change involved and how it would affect you, or were you unaware of the change for some time? If you were, what information did you want and how did you get the information you wanted, or did you guess and find out the hard way–by experiencing the reality?

Q4. To what extent were your views asked for or, if volunteered, considered? Did you have a voice that was heard, and if so, how did that affect your feelings about the change?

Q5. What happened in the lead up to the actual change occurring in terms of information, incidents, your thinking and feeling? To what extent did you feel in control or controlled? When the change appeared on the horizon, did that alter your previous attitude and behaviour? If so, how and why?

During the event

Q6. When the actual event took place, what were your thoughts and feelings, and, if the event was expected, how did the actual experience compare with your expectations? Better or worse, and why?

After the event

Q7. How did the actual event impact subsequently on your thinking and feeling, attitude and behaviour? Looking back, what permanent changes occurred, and what do you think were the key reasons for those changes? What, in short, do you think you have learned from the experience? If your initial emotional response was negative, how much, if any, of that feeling remains, and can you think of any positive aspects that have occurred and why? Equally, if your immediate emotional response was positive, how much of that feeling remains, and can you think of any negative aspects and why?

Q8. Finally, if you were offering advice from your experience and reflection on that experience on how people could maximize the learning from change, what advice would you give, and why?

Reactions

I hope you found that useful. Let us look at some common change situations, how individuals reacted to them, what they learned and how learning is affected by their change profile. I shall use the words they used when filling in the questionnaire. Again, all the names have been changed.

Julia

The event: Being fired from my first job after leaving college.

Q6–During the event: Shocked, humiliated, complete disbelief.

Q7–After the event: Still feel very negative about it—because he would not ask me for any 'feedback' or justification for my behaviour. I am still convinced he still thinks the worse of me, and as the reasons for sacking had no foundation, this rankles.

If I had to meet him today, I would want to explain, but still I don't think he would listen or even be capable of understanding.

Learnt not to trust people as a result, and still occasionally lack confidence in ability. Have since learnt that, had the two of us communicated better, all of this could have been avoided. We were both naive—my first job—his first time with staff in his business.

Q8–Advice on learning from change:

- Not to take it personally.
- If I had known what he was thinking!
- Tell people what and why and get emotions out of the way first.
- Tell the truth—don't lie.

Julia's profile is:

LD	NC	PF	PC
19	31	**36**	34

The key factors in the profile are the above average NC and below average LD. The emotional modes are 67 compared with the intellectual modes of 53, a significant gap of 14. It is interesting that Julia's learning was to be honest to her emotions and express them early on.

As I have discovered when analysing the responses, our learning from change often gives a clue to our own profiles. We should not suppress emotion, and to gain effective growth out of change, the emotional aspects have to be dealt with.

However, with the low LD, Julia fails to consider the consequence of an instant and inevitably negative emotional response. Remember, a high NC does imply a self-centred approach, though the strong PF compensates.

There is a danger of aggression if we simply try to assert our rights—in this case the right to express our feelings. True assertiveness is a mutuality approach, where we recognize and react to others' rights as well as our own. This is exemplified in Chapter 5.

If we effectively understand the logical and emotional position of the other person, and display that knowledge effectively to him or her, we are in a strong position to gain his or her understanding of our position, and move towards a genuine dialogue which combines the LD/LC or intellectual modes.

Julia's story shows how sudden change, which is perceived as negative, can lead to initial (and sometimes permanent) disbelief. If we move beyond disbelief, as most of us do, there is an inevitable negative emotional reaction that has to be managed. Part of that response is to blame both externally and internally, which reduces our self-confidence and self-esteem. This is something else that needs to be recognized and managed (see Chapter 5).

The extent and duration of the negative phase is not the same for all of us. A key factor is the development level at which we are operating when the event takes place. This will be examined in Chapter 4. Finally, as profiles and development levels are connected, a strong bias in our profile can impact on outcomes.

There can be an element of cause and effect. A near traumatic change, especially when we are young, can create a profile with a 'naturally' high NC. It may take years to shift that. Again, this is exemplified in Chapter 5. If we have developed a strong orientation as a result of experience, then that will tend to dictate how we respond to change, and whether we initiate change.

As the respondent said at the beginning: 'It did highlight for me how we repeat processes in situations totally different to that which inspired the internal model.'

No human being is cast in concrete (unless he or she has fallen foul of the Mafia!). Self-knowledge, recognition of how we are likely to respond and why—combined with a desire to change and knowing what to do, and actually doing it—will lead to incremental improvement in time and change over time.

Incidentally, some of you may be disturbed or even offended by what has hitherto been an implicit statement: you need to change. I do not intend offence. However, if you genuinely want to create personal growth out of change, then staying as you are will not achieve that result. Change of a discontinuous nature is undesirable and a low probability, but change that is incremental and connected to the present and the past—i.e. improvement—will be necessary.

Finally, on a lighter note I would reinforce a key message that sudden change should be avoided when we are *initiating* change, i.e. in proactive mode.

EXAMPLE

A man is on a long vacation, and receives a letter from his friend. (We will assume this location has no telephones.) The letter baldly states that his beloved cat Tiddles is dead. The man is very upset, and writes back to his friend to complain at the unkind way she told him the sad news. He suggests that she should have let him know gradually, with a series of communications.

For instance, she could write first of all that the cat had climbed onto the roof. Next, perhaps, that the cat had slipped on the roof, then that the cat had fallen off the roof, then that the cat had injured himself, then that the injury was quite serious, then that it was very serious, then that it was touch and go, and finally that the cat had died.

His friend wrote to apologize profusely and agreed that she should have proceeded as suggested. A few weeks later, his friend wrote to advise him that his mother-in-law had climbed onto the roof!

Charles

The event: Being unexpectedly asked to join the board in my last organization, a PLC. It was during a period of considerable turmoil and change.

Q1—Prior to the event: It took place immediately, so mental preparation was not possible.

Q2—Source of information and feeling: The MD (managing director) was the sole source. Felt flattered, shocked, concerned and to some extent inadequate and maybe not up to the job; certainly elated.

Q3—What the change involved: Somewhat in the dark as a reorganization was placed around the new position. (It also involved a culture change.) Largely in the deep end. In my first two weeks, the MD went on holiday and not only was I managing three departments, he wanted me to produce a report on a possible takeover of another organization. I felt he was using me.

Q4—Your views considered: The MD produced a plan with the FD (finance director). The plan was unworkable but the senior management were not given the opportunity to input to the plan. I felt stressed and in an impossible position quite quickly. The writing of the plan was all that was needed to produce the required results!!!

Q5–The lead up and change in attitude: The 'Old guard' of 25 years standing were sacked by institutional shareholders. The new team had a simplified view of the group's position, which produced naive decisions, which could not work. We were controlled and criticism was not tolerated. As the situation grew worse, the MD moved harder and harder to a very directive leadership style, because of his personal fear of the future. I became more stressed.

Q6–During the event: On joining the board I felt that the plan might just be possible. On being exposed to the thinking at board meetings genuine concern and frustration quickly took over. The outcome was worse in the end. I was 'muzzled' before board meetings with the non-executive directors present. The situation deteriorated to the extent that I resigned to the MD, who accepted my resignation. He was then fired by the chairman, who asked me to come back!

Q7–After the event: What I didn't know was the chairman (a 'city' man) had never approved of my role, declaring it 'impossible'. When I resigned, he was furious because the MD had never passed on my misgivings.

My emotions swung from 'failure and resignation' to 'positive and thank God for that'. Failure was something new for me, and, if the chairman had not stepped in, I would have had significant self-doubt over my ability to implement change.

Looking back, I would be considerably more assertive in the earlier stages. This assertion is always tempered with a feeling of 'I didn't know for certain' or the ever hopeful 'it is possible'.

Q8–Advice on learning from change

- Don't accept another plan without much work and 2-way discussion–analyse.
- Form relationships with all the key players and find out the full picture and context of the change.
- Don't be assumptive on the issues surrounding the change.
- Find out the hidden agendas.
- Demand thinking time.
- Look to your instincts and act on them.
- Have confidence in your ability to contribute.
- Change inflicted is much harder to deliver.

Charles's profile is:

LD	NC	PF	PC
23	20	**40**	37

The example here is of sudden change, perceived as positive. The suddenness triggers an emotional rather than an intellectual response, as is always the case.

There are the positive emotions of feeling flattered and elated, but because the suddenness produces uncertainty, there are also instant emotions of shock (not far from disbelief) and slight inadequacy. We are simply not logical if change is sudden and we need to recognize this.

This is why 'demanding thinking time' is so essential, so that we can control our emotions and ensure that we start finding facts (LD) and uncovering and questioning assumptions (PC).

On the relationship side, the need to be assertive is stressed as a key learning point.

Charles's profile indicates a combination of a positive and questioning approach, coupled with the need to give support to others involved. The questionnaire does not ask whether you supported others, but it is interesting to note that the chairman certainly felt supported by Charles. When push came to shove, the MD was pushed and not Charles.

The comment on the MD's leadership style is worth highlighting. As covered in the first chapter, change, where we perceive we have no control, produces uncertainty. Uncertainty produces fear—fear of the unknown. Fear pulls us down, and reduces our capacity to gain growth out of change.

If we are frightened, we try to overcome our fear by controlling our environment—we move strongly into NC mode. In terms of leadership style, we become more and more directive, less capable of providing support (PF) or encouraging creativity (PC).

We therefore increase the probability of failure of our organizations, as we deny ourselves and those we lead the capacity for growth, and leave only the reality of regression.

It is a sad truth that because of leadership reaction to recession, many more companies went to the wall than needed to. Tom Peters in his video 'Recession as opportunity' postulated in 1989, before the recession had taken hold in the US, that six out of seven companies would regress to the 'animal'—savage cost-cutting, no employee involvement nor consultation, and rule by the rod of fear. As a result, he suggested, they would be in a very weak position to get growth out of recovery. Trust, generated over a decade, would be destroyed in a few weeks.

Who cares wins!

It is worth highlighting the value of the NC mode as well as its associated problems. Being locked into NC is bad, but that is true of any mode. Also, NC tends to be a basic level mode, to which we regress with sudden unpleasant change, and from which we need to progress into other modes, if we are to gain growth out of change (see the next chapter).

However, NC is a necessary, inevitable reality, because we are human. We need to recognize that reality in ourselves and others; we also need to recognize the need in ourselves and others to gain control of uncertain environments, and for emotional support, when we have lost our core of comfort.

If we return to the recession, that provides a case in point. It is necessary to move into aspects of NC, because an NC approach in organizational terms means being conservative, cautious, cutting back, and retrenchment–all of which is necessary when that is exactly what is happening in the external environment.

An NC approach with a PF/LD/PC leadership style is a great combination. As Tom Peters said: 'touch decisions must be made'. Where the problem is shared with the employees (PF) who are encouraged to suggest creative new approaches (PC) and empowered to take rational decisions (LD), this beats 'control and cut' hands down.

CASE STUDY

A small US manufacturing company was hit hard by the recession. They had to cut costs or increase sales in tough market conditions. Many production workers were idle. What should they do? The board posed the problem to the factory workers, expecting them to decide on pay cuts or redundancy.

The factory workers decided to go for growth through selling. They were hungry for their jobs, and they knew the product backwards. So they organized teams, followed existing completed orders for repeat business, and started prospecting for new business, where the existing salesforce were not involved.

They outsold the salesforce and saved their jobs.

Equally, too little NC and too much PC in a leader's profile can cause problems.

EXAMPLE

There was a managing director of a small UK financial services company with a low NC and high PC, and moderate PF and LD. By taking risks, being opportunistic, he got great growth out of the good times.

But what do you think happened when the bad times came?

First of all, he did not recognize them until long after their arrival. Then he thought that more ideas, more marketing, more selling, more technology, different approaches, and more staff would do the trick.

It did not.

No problem. He then decided to have masses of change—new structures, new roles, new responsibilities, new ideas, more marketing, more selling, more technology, new approaches, and more staff. That should do the trick.

It did not.

No, NC is not bad; it is how we deal with NC that causes problems.

Marion

The event: Change in position at place of employment.

Q1–Prior to the event: I had no suspicion, and it was perhaps due to extreme naivety on my part that this was a possibility I had never envisaged as long as the organization survived.

Q2–Source of information and feeling: My line manager. My immediate response was unhappy disbelief and–overdramatic though it sounds–betrayal.

Q3–What the change involved: The fact that my position within the company was to change radically was immediately apparent, shortly followed by the realization that this would impact in due course upon my potential grading when the parent organization's new scheme was introduced, and therefore my salary and eventual pension. Job security was also an issue suddenly to be considered.

As far as information about my new job was concerned, both the individuals concerned made an opportunity early on to explain what would be involved. While this was appreciated subsequently, at the time I seemed to be functioning in a cloud of such wretchedness and confusion that I was incapable of responding and was, indeed, resentful of the speed with which the ramifications of this unwanted move were being thrust upon me.

Q4–Your views considered: At no time was there any consultation regarding the change itself, nor was my opinion sought about any aspect of it. It was clear that the decision had been based in part upon assumptions intended to be viewed as having my interests at heart, but no attempt was made to seek verification of these.

During the few days following its announcement, I was asked frequently by my colleagues how I felt but I realized that the expression of a negative view, which was all that I was experiencing at the time, would serve no purpose and only embarrass my listener. It was therefore expedient, except with a very few colleagues, to assume an act.

Q5–The lead up and change in attitude: Within days of my being advised of the change, I was required to begin a programme of instructing my successor. This was pushed by management and I did feel 'controlled'. I would have liked a little longer to get used to the idea, particularly as I had no heart for handing over!

In over seven years I had made the job my own, creating most of the systems and building up sound relationships with colleagues, and I did not like accepting that I would no longer occupy a key role in the organization and could not look for anything like comparable fulfilment in my new task.

It was a real effort to assume a bright, positive exterior in order to be as fair as possible to my replacement, for whom I had respect and a good deal of sympathy for her own sudden and unexpected 'transplant'.

Q6–During the event: For some weeks following the change I continued to feel hurt and rejected. I have been fortunate in finding myself now with two extremely caring people who share my values and whose own approach to working circumstances has done much to put my experience into its rightful perspective; for the intensity of my feelings had surprised myself and was a matter of concern to me, when viewed alongside what I know to be of real importance.

Q7–After the event: I believe that the main change that has occurred as a result of this experience is one of attitude, and to that extent the episode may be seen as beneficial, the business world being as it is. I no longer feel the deep loyalty to the establishment that formerly resulted in hours of unacknowledged overtime, given happily enough when I could believe I was valued; and I have deliberately cultivated an 'it's just a job' philosophy which I hope will serve me well should a similar situation occur in the future.

Q8–Advice on learning from change: The one clear lesson I have derived from this experience is not to assume anything! I believe that if I had been made more aware of my vulnerability rather than–apparently too readily–believing my colleague's kind observations over the years about my 'indispensability' and 'unique suitability' to the role, the blow would not have been quite so resounding!

There is one golden rule, which is not an original thought of mine, for those of us who initiate change, who care, but all too often do not think enough before we act.

> *Never implement a change on another person until we have thought and tried to feel how we would respond to the same change imposed on us in the same way.*

If we don't like it, then change it.

The above response explains Tom Peter's pessimistic view for those organizations that go the 'animal' route.

With trust gone, and work effectiveness diminished (and that multiplied to an organizational level), where will the growth come from? Put differently, recovery means opportunity. How many 'Marions' will leave if they get the chance?

Marion's profile:

LD	NC	PF	PC
18	34	**39**	29

The care shines through–putting on a face so as not to upset colleagues, training her successor well and with a positive face, even though bleeding inside.

The high NC that was probably increased by this event also comes through, especially in the 'learning'.

Callum

The event: My first change of company after seven years with the same employers from graduation.

Q1–Prior to the event: One of my friends and colleagues, a compulsive 'job-hunter', left the company to join another. He spoke in high terms of them in contrast to my company. I saw a job advert for his new company and applied.

Though I was offered the job, I declined it as I was offered a significant (first time managerial promotion) with my existing employer. But the dog had seen a rabbit. The thought that I could move dawned and led to a growing frustration. The idea of a change of environment, industry, location, and peer group became increasingly attractive, but I did nothing about it.

Two years later, the new company phoned me and asked me to meet their MD to discuss joining them in a more senior role still. Over a period of two months a deal was agreed and I made my first change of company.

Q2–Source of information and feeling: Source of information–largely personal contacts. Feelings of anticipation, excitement and challenge on the one hand, balanced with a fear of the comparatively unknown; nervousness at making a 'leap in the dark'. Absolutely delighted, when the job was offered (I had 'won'); terror at the thought, 'God, what have I done–in leaving "security" for grass that looked greener?'

Q3–What the change involved: I saw the change in broad terms and had not thought through (or even realized) the implications. The approach was reactive and I was coached through it by friends, family and other colleagues. My confidence had been boosted to a dangerous level and 'reality' took some time to truly impinge. I dived in too fast, and thought, reflected and planned too little.

Q4–Your views considered: I felt very much in control, though the reality was rather different! This was not a change that was imposed. I felt flattered that my existing employer tried to keep me, while my new employer wanted me on board very fast and kept providing extra incentives to speed the process. I felt very much in demand and my views and opinions were widely sought. Talk about an ego trip!

Q5–The lead up and change in attitude: The run up to the decision was very exciting and stimulating. Once the decision was finalized, there was a period of flatness–a transfer of power as my 'old' job was taken, a feeling of uselessness during the (shortened) notice period, an exclusion from areas of habitual operation.

From being/feeling indispensable, the reality of being dispensable dawned. Anticipation of benefits from the change kept me going. The interregnum was uncomfortable, unanticipated–internally balanced by splendid support from customers and 'external' contacts who gave a better perspective.

Q6–During the event: The transition was long and slow. The culture was very different–more aggression, thrusting and entrepreneurial. The market was closer and making demands to which the response was to be positive–*can do* rather than the previous *can't do*. I found it much harder to change and adapt than I had thought. The habits of seven years were no longer appropriate. The scale of the required change was huge and I lacked the frameworks reference to anchor me.

Q7–After the event: Looking back, this change was a vital experience. The feelings at the time were mixed. Emotionally, it 'shocked' away feelings of complacency and comfort. It made me much more open and adaptable to further change; more confident, based on the ability to cope and to initiate change rather than react/resist it; more measured in looking at my own feelings and motivation and sensing others' feelings; more flexible as a team player capable of influencing upwards.

Q8–Advice on learning from change: People are only as adaptable and as flexible as they allow themselves to be. Most have greater capability than they realize and are often shackled by habits without realizing the constraining effect on their thinking. It can become insidious. In my case, the experience of change blasted away the 'mind forged shackles', and led to a view that change is a vital part of development to be actively sought. Status quo is an unnatural state. The one 'fixed' point is that of continual change.

It will come as no surprise to the reader that Callum's profile has a strong PC!

Callum's profile:

LD	NC	PF	PC
28	23	31	**38**

This response is interesting, because it is the first case in which the change was voluntarily sought. The NC is now quite low, but would have been higher at the time, as implied by Callum. After seven years with the same employer, there is bound to be a reluctance or resistance to change, that is purely voluntary.

The first bite at the cherry was refused, but the confidence, gained from the offer, led to increasing dissatisfaction with the status quo. Even so, Callum was reactive and not proactive—he was approached again, and this time (after two months) took the bait.

I am not surprised that the LD is quite high, as there can be a competitive element associated with LD, and Callum would appear to be competitive.

This story reinforces the message of the weak joke, but from a different perspective. When initiating rather than reacting to change, a gradual approach is likely to have the greatest success. Just as a friend should prepare us gradually for bad news, so too should we prepare ourselves gradually for good news we create. Momentum, which is gradually built, will have a lasting effect when it has overcome inertia and created the change.

Another point reinforces the 'unpredictability' reality of change. As the consequences of change can never be predicted in advance, Callum's message of flexibility and adaptability is a key one. Without planning, without preparing, we ask ourselves to leap in the dark. That is unwise as well as uncomfortable. But if we become too comfortable, too certain, and fail to recognize that the map is not reality, then we can lose out—be surprised and disappointed by the unexpected, which is inevitable.

One final point before we move on. In a world of change, perhaps it is wise to develop an acceptance of change mentality, as Callum clearly has. In fact, he has gone farther. For Callum, change is the key to growth—the only fixed point—hence the low NC that a positive experience of change produces.

There is a balance, I feel. There is a richness in continuity, as well as wealth from change. If we always fix on the future and change, can we ever be satisfied in the present? D.H. Lawrence defined death in one of his poems as peace—the absence of questioning that was life. Perhaps, sometimes, we need that kind of death in life.

Carla

The event: Starting first job, straight after leaving college.

Q1—Prior to the event: Was advised of the position after reading advertisement in a magazine.

Q2—Source of information and feeling: Lecturers at college, advertisement in magazine; felt excited; first job that had attracted my interest—also felt apprehensive—setting wheels in motion if I applied—could become less in control of my life/lifestyle.

Q3—What the change involved: Was fairly uncertain about what the change would entail—had a pretty good idea about what the job itself entailed—but other aspects such as accommodation, social life, clubs, etc. had to be found out the hard way: found I left things to the last minute and then just took things as they came. I think I learned more by experiencing the reality.

Q4—Your views considered: My views were pretty much asked for. There was quite a lot of consideration about my views and what I wanted. Consequently I felt pretty happy about the change and confident that I'd made the correct decision for me.

Q5—The lead up and change in attitude: I think, to a certain extent, I felt I was being controlled, e.g. going through selection procedures, etc. Was told to do certain things and found myself doing them without questioning them. Information was freely offered and sought by myself. Don't think my actual behaviour changed too much.

Q6—During the event: Pretty smooth transition really—suddenly felt in control of myself and my lifestyle—knew that I had made a good decision and had taken the right step on the career ladder.

Q7—After the event: Positive feelings are no longer as strong as they were, partly due to the fact that I have done it! I moved away from the safe environment of college and into the world at large and did it successfully and confidently and now need another change to challenge myself.

Q8—Advice on learning from change: To trust instincts and to experience reality—to go it alone but never be afraid of asking for help/advice/info and trust in that advice. To use experiences positively, wherever possible.

I like Carla's change experience, as it is positive, and confirms some of the basic points for gaining growth out of change.
    Carla's profile:

LD	NC	PF	PC
25	24	**36**	**35**

As I have said, there is always uncertainty associated with change. But if we initiate change—are proactive (where we have a choice) rather than reactive—the uncertainty is bound to be less. If we ask questions, explore, seek information and get answers, ask and get support, and feel that our views are respected and are taken into account, then uncertainty diminishes, our perception of retaining control expands and our confidence grows. If we have given our trust and feel in control, we are more prepared to yield control—a vital point in effective leadership, covered in the next chapter.

If we are positive and excited, and experience growth out of change, then our natural curiosity and desire to grow further leads to dissatisfaction with the new status quo, and the need to seek another change to challenge ourselves.

A final true story of how one young woman, we shall call her Jackie, managed to gain growth out of sudden, negative change. Jackie was an assistant fee earner (i.e. a newly qualified solicitor processing work for a partner) in a City Law firm with little management skills or systems, facing a crisis because of enormous reductions in earnings. **CASE STUDY**

Jackie had just received an 8 per cent pay rise (!) on the back of a good appraisal a couple of weeks earlier. One morning, she was called in to see one of the partners she worked for. He looked harassed and very uncomfortable. He told her that they would have to let her go, as her work was not up to standard.

Jackie pointed out that she had just had a good appraisal, so what on earth was he talking about? Did he mean that her work had deteriorated in the past two weeks? Initially, he mumbled 'Yes', but when asked to provide evidence, he backtracked.

'But you are still giving me the sack', she enquired, 'even though my work is up to standard?'. 'No, no', he replied. 'So, what are you saying to me?' 'Nothing, nothing. Just make sure you keep up to scratch', and he walked hurriedly out of his own office.

Later that day, Jackie was summoned to see the partner responsible for personnel, who told her that she was, in fact, 'being let go'. Jackie asked what sort of severance package she would get. The personnel partner replied: 'Nothing.' Jackie stated strongly that the whole business had been shamefully handled. She ought to be paid some redundancy money, and she supposed, she would just have to go to the industrial relations tribunal. Visibly taken aback, the partner offered her six months' salary in the form of a tax-free redundancy.

Jackie gratefully accepted, and may still, at the time you read this book, be travelling round the world. The sum of money was around £20 000!

As Jackie had been employed for less than two years, she was legally entitled to receive the initial offer—nothing!

A remarkable young woman who controlled her emotions well and used a logical, assertive and questioning approach to gain a substantial windfall.

Key point summary

■ Sudden change produces an emotional and not logical response.

■ If the change is perceived negatively, there will be an initial disbelief, followed by negative emotions towards others and self.

■ We should consciously try to control our emotions until we have questioned our own assumptions and those of others, fully understood the nature and implications and considered how we can improve the outcome. 'The head must rule the heart, before the heart rules the head.'

■ It is important that we identify and understand the position of the person initiating the change, and display our understanding to that individual.

■ When the change is perceived positively, there will be negative as well as positive feelings, due to the 'uncertainty' aspect of change. These should be recognized, acknowledged and managed.

■ When initiating change for ourselves, we should plan carefully, implement gradually, but be flexible in what we expect as the outcome. This is necessary, owing to the 'unpredictability' aspect of change—the actual change as it occurs and is completed will never be as planned.

■ When contemplating change for others, we should consider carefully how we would react in their shoes, and plan to remove any negative reactions we anticipate.

■ From an organizational perspective, a cautious approach to change is natural, as is a controlling leadership style. But leaders should recognize the value of involving staff in problem-solving and decision-taking. This will help retain trust in the bad times, which, if destroyed, will not readily return in the good times, and so deny or limit the ability to gain growth out of recovery.

Your own points

Your action plan

Development levels and leadership

Introduction

We have looked at the dimensions of change, and the dilemma of change as well as considering how we can get personal growth out of change, using the learning cycle, the learning ladder and action planning. You have produced your change preference profile, and have discovered the meaning for you, helped by the analysis of the profiles of other individuals.

Next, you completed a questionnaire, which enabled you to examine a significant experience of change in your past, reflect on the impact over time, and distil what for you was the key learning. Through considering other people's responses to business situations, we have uncovered some of the automatic emotional responses to sudden change, how profiles are determined by historic change, how they affect response to future change and the ability to initiate effective change.

We have also uncovered some basic strategies for improving our own response to change, for initiating change, and helping others through change.

In this chapter, we examine the concept of development levels, which has been mentioned in earlier chapters. We also look briefly and pragmatically at leadership, as that is a vital role in our business environments. By improving our competence, we improve our ability to implement change effectively and manage necessary change in others.

Leaders in an environment of change are also agents of change. It is a vital role often not fully appreciated by those who hold leadership positions. More hold such positions in organizations than recognize it. If you share a secretary, you are a leader and an agent of change.

Finally, we link leadership to development level.

Development levels

The concept of development levels is based on Abraham Maslow's hierarchy of needs, as modified by Roger Harrison, an expert on culture and change. I have focused on change and development, and synthesized Maslow and Harrison to produce four levels of development rather than five levels of need. I call these *survival, security, self-esteem* and *growth*.

There are two important points about development levels in the context of change:

■ Where we are will impact on how we manage change.

■ Traumatic change will push us down a level or two.

These points are considered in detail in the next chapter, 'Reacting to change'.

Another important point is that few of us fit wholly into one category. We can have aspects of one mixed with aspects of another in a dynamic way. In fact, as we go through our daily activities, we demonstrate behaviours, reflecting different levels as we react to or initiate different changes. We also tend to show a behavioural orientation over time, which reflects where we are overall in terms of development level.

Let us look first of all at each of the four levels shown in Figures 4.1–4.4.

Survival

This is the basic animal level, reflecting the basic survival needs, satisfied for most but not all people living in developed countries. However, we have whole populations in Africa and elsewhere locked in the battle to survive. We have individuals in this country, the homeless as an example, who live in survival mode. We also have an example of regression, where people who were operating at higher levels have descended down and down into the dark—e.g. Bosnia.

Humanity can indeed be a fragile flower.

Bosnia is also an example of a sexual difference. Generally speaking, it is almost impossible to move into higher levels of development when fighting to survive. But humanity can transcend the animal or there is in nature a form of growth—the ultimate gift of one's own life, which many women and a few men have given so that the children survive and they do not.

Security

If our survival needs have been met, we move to level 2—gaining security. Eric Erikson has developed Maslow into the concept of development being associated with the ageing process. With that perspective, security would be very much a function of childhood. For many that may be true, but for many it is not.

Figure 4.1 *Development level 1: Survival.*

Figure 4.2 *Development level 2: Security.*

Figure 4.3   *Development level 3: Self-esteem.*

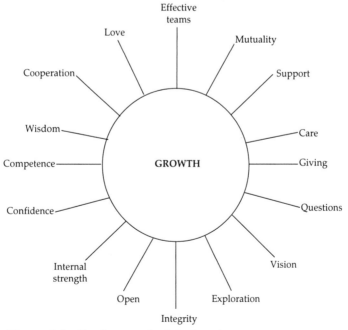

Figure 4.4   *Development level 4: Growth.*

For some, adult life becomes a search, whether conscious or not, for satisfaction of the needs for security, particularly emotional security, not met in children. When we are children we have a strong need for security. But so too when we are grown up, as reflected in our change preference assessment.

Even if we are operating at a higher level, the needs of a lower level lie dormant to be awakened at any time. It is noticeable today how many managers and executives, when asked to select and prioritize what motivates them (an indication of development level), have placed job security at the top of the list. Many more than did so before the recession.

Self-esteem

This is the level at which most of us spend much of our time. There will be aspects of security in our lives, and aspects of the next level—growth. This is the level at which we are trying to build our self-esteem and confidence; the level at which we seek responsibility, strive to achieve, like to increase our material wealth, desire recognition, and so on.

There will be a different focus for different people as value systems and circumstances vary. There may also be gender differences: more men than women seek self-esteem through a focus on task, and more women than men through a focus on relationships.

Growth

This is the highest level. This is where our needs to survive have been met; where our needs for security have been met; and where we have self-esteem—we respect and appreciate ourselves. This is the level at which we can truly give, not receive; where we can effectively help others to develop and build their competence and confidence; where we are part of effective teams and not social groups; where we let go because we do not need to hold on; where we explore, ask questions, seek answers—and grow.

Having looked at each level, I would now like to link in the four change modes LD, NC, PF and PC as shown in Tables 4.1 and 4.2.

Table 4.1 Development levels and change modes

Level	Primary mode	Focus
1. Survival	NC	Internal
2. Security	NC/LD	Internal
3. Self-esteem	NC/LD/PF/PC	Internal and external
4. Growth	PF/PC	External

Table 4.2 Development levels and leadership

Level	Leadership provided and needed
2. Security	'Command and control'
	↓
	'Control with support'
3. Self-esteem	↓
	'Support with control'
4. Growth	'Questioning coach' 'Visionary team'

- When at the survival level (1) the primary mode is raw NC.

- When operating at the security level (2), the combination is NC and LD–internal and closed.

- When developing self-esteem (3), all modes are present, though the NC/LD combination weakens the higher we progress.

- At the highest level of growth (4) the primary combination is PF/PC–an external orientation. That does not mean to say that we become illogical. Logic–rational rather than irrational thinking–analysis and evaluation would be present at the growth level, but as an 'unconscious competence'. The focus would be PF/PC. We would have lost the irrational or prejudicial logic that supports an NC mode and closes down thought and exploration.

This logical 'unconscious competence' is very noticeable in effective teams. Much of the time is spent in exploration, and decision-making is very quick, a reflection of the empathy and bonding that exists between individuals. I cover teams in Chapter 8, but it is worth emphasizing that *the team is probably the single most powerful force, enabling the individual to give and receive personal growth out of change.*

Before we move on, I would mention the NC/PC combination, which is a very powerful and dangerous combination. You could call it the 'Van Gogh' combination–living simultaneously at the highest and lowest levels, by-passing the intermediate phases. As we know, such a combination produces great art and great discoveries at the cost of enormous personal pain. Finally, there can be a PC element, when we are in survival mode: 'Necessity is the mother of invention'.

Let us consider a few types of behaviour where we demonstrate, and determine, the development level at which we are operating. Explicit recognition of the link and conscious thought can raise the development level, even if only temporarily.

Criticism

Criticism is in fact a security behaviour *and* a self-esteem behaviour, which is why there is a lot of blame, fault-finding and buck-passing in many cultures. When we are explicitly criticizing someone else, we can be implicitly building our self-esteem. The logic goes like this:

Explicitly or consciously: 'You have a fault, which I am pointing out to you, because I want you to eradicate it, and grow as a result. In fact, I am a caring human being and you should be grateful for my helpful intervention.'

Implicitly or subconsciously: 'Great. I have found someone with a fault I don't have. I'll tell her off. That'll make her look inferior to me and I superior to her. This will build my self-esteem, which is very important to me.'

However, we may be at the security level, in which case, the subconscious comment will be:

'I have a fault, which I can never consciously recognize in myself, as it would make me feel too insecure. So what I'll do instead is tell people I meet that *they* have the fault, whether they do or not, and if I tell enough people sufficiently frequently, maybe my fault will go away.'

The NC/LD combination can produce irrational or prejudicial thought!

The absence of criticism is the mark of someone operating at the growth development level. It is interesting that, in effective teams, there is an absence of criticism. Instead, there is feedback, dialogue, exploration and discovery—a PF/PC focus with rational LD.

Sarcasm is a very close relative of criticism!

Seeking praise

Clearly, we seek praise to build our self-esteem. That is very natural. If someone shows an excess of this behaviour, then it indicates security needs rather than self-esteem.

Giving praise (where it is due) is a growth behaviour—it helps to build people's self-esteem or reduce their insecurity, and so improves their confidence.

Listening

Listening is potentially a growth behaviour *if* it is active and effective. The key conditions for this are:

- Concentration and focus on the speaker—emptying our heads of our own thoughts and concerns that usually fill them.

- The right 'body language'—sitting still (not fidgeting nor 'pencil-tapping'), an open posture (arms not folded nor behind the head, and the back at or near the vertical), good, warm eye contact (no eye-balling nor staring out of the window) and the occasional nod or helpful murmur.

- Feedback to confirm understanding: 'So let me see. You think that we should …'

- No judgement during the act.

If we succeed, we convey the message to the speaker that we think that he or she *and* what he or she has to say are important to us and are valued by us.

Questioning

The way we question people is a very good indication of our development level at that particular moment. If we use a *closed, judgemental* approach, we are exercising control (security level) or building self-esteem through criticism.

- 'Logic dictates that this is the only viable approach. Don't you agree?'

- 'I am with the chairman on this one. What about you?'

- 'No sensible person would spend much time on a trivial report like this one. What do you think?'

- 'Surely you do not have any doubts about our new mission?'

- 'Do you not agree that John's time-keeping is poor?'

If we use short, open questions, that indicates growth level.

- 'What do you think, George?'

- 'So tell me, what was the highlight of the evening?'

- 'How do you feel about the proposal?'

- 'Any ideas?'

One open question of the set of six—how, what, why, when, where, who— causes a lot of trouble. Can you work out which one it is and why?

Why haven't you worked it out?

'Why' is the cause of many genuine misunderstandings in many relationships! On the surface, it is the basic rational question—to uncover the facts needed for good decisions. As such it is an exemplary question. It is often intended in that capacity by the questioner, but it is not always received in the spirit in which it was intended. The receiver reads in implied criticism, and reacts accordingly. What was intended to spark rational, logical debate ends up producing irrational, argument.

'Why' should therefore be used with considerable discretion and replaced where possible, or deliberately off-set in its potential impact by the prelude to the question.

■ 'It would help me understand the situation better, if you would give me your reasons for doing this.'

■ 'That's an interesting suggestion. Why do you think it's the best way forward?'

■ 'What do you think were or will be the consequences?'

■ 'So, please tell me the assumptions you made when doing this.'

■ 'How did the "third party" react when you did that?'

If you have time, you can use the balanced feedback approach, which is a good example of coaching.

■ 'What went well and why?'

and

■ 'What could have been improved and how?'

Leadership

There is a common view on what good leaders do and what they need to do to be effective. This view crosses hierarchies and cultures. *It is your view* and is therefore worth sharing.

On many programmes run by Sundridge Park in the UK and overseas for top executives through to middle managers, the same views are expressed. We ask individuals to share their thoughts on leadership in small groups. Specifically, they consider their personal experience of leadership during their business lives. They identify the positive or negative actions and behaviours that they experienced from those leaders. More importantly, they identify the reasons for these actions and behaviours. By pooling and discussing these views, we obtain a picture of what the *client* wants from a good leader.

What better definition of leadership than that provided by the led?

There is a large core of common views, that transcend culture and status. I shall share with you the views expressed by 18 executives (varying from senior managers, functional and line directors through to a managing director and a chief executive officer) working for Renong Group, a Malaysian company that focuses on running hotels, and building and managing roads. I do not deviate from the agreed summary, and use the discussion that took place.

Good leaders

The Renong view of good leadership can be seen from the following list:

- Think explicitly about the leadership role.

- Develop self-awareness and self-belief.

- Focus externally: listen, support, provide feedback and coach.

- Display integrity in decision-taking and take decisions.

- Share information.

- Be confident enough to make mistakes, admit mistakes and learn from mistakes.

- Direct with coaching.

- Delegate authority as well as responsibility.

Think explicitly about their leadership role

One of the reasons identified in poor leadership was thoughtlessness. It was recognized that abruptness or inadequate briefings, or being left to twiddle your thumbs while your boss chatted on the telephone, was rarely a deliberate insult or meant that the 'subordinate' was held in low esteem. It was simply the result of thoughtlessness.

As mentioned in the Introduction, we do not spend much, if any, time explicitly thinking of ourselves as leaders or agents of change. We may wrestle with a complex technical or task issue, plan to deal with an awkward client, prepare for a presentation, think long and hard about a report we are writing and how we are going to sell it, but we spend little time thinking about the leadership role that we perform much of the time.

So good leaders think about their leadership role and plan their leadership strategy in much the same way as they do for all these other important matters.

Develop self-awareness and self-belief

Poor leaders display an excess of control, usually because they either need to control or want to control. Debate in this instance focused on need, which was perceived as arising fundamentally from uncertainty. The identified sources of uncertainty were the individuals themselves and/or changes in the business environment. A lack of security and self-belief could be subconscious and, therefore, difficult to deal with owing to lack of recognition.

Good leaders developed an awareness of self. They identified, acknowledged and understood their strengths and weaknesses, believed in themselves and in their competence and capability. Leaders had to think positively about themselves, before they could think positively about those they led. The more they were in control of themselves, the less they needed to control others.

Focus externally: listen, support, provide feedback and coach

Poor leaders focus on themselves. By developing self-awareness and self-belief, and by becoming comfortable with themselves, good leaders could do what those being led wanted—focus on the follower.

Good leaders were good listeners, providing support at both the logical and emotional levels, and providing feedback to encourage their followers and enable them to develop. Finally, good leaders were good coaches: they asked the awkward questions that enabled the followers to discover and learn for themselves rather than being told what to do.

Display integrity in decision-taking and take decisions

Some poor leaders took bad and inconsistent decisions to accommodate the changing power shifts in the body politic or the changing views of those in command. Others took no decisions and 'delegated' them down by default to avoid offending anyone adversely affected by the decision.

Share information

Jan Carlson of Scandinavian Airlines made the remark that: 'An individual without information cannot take responsibility: an individual with information cannot help but take responsibility.'

Good leaders recognized that their followers wanted responsibility and so shared information. They operated a 'need to know' policy from the follower and not the organizational perspective.

Be confident enough to make mistakes, admit mistakes and learn from mistakes

Poor leaders denied learning and effective problem-solving to themselves and their followers because they needed to be perceived as infallible.

The word *confidence* was first used here. That is the outcome of self-awareness and self-belief, allied with the humility to recognize that capability does not mean infallibility, and that change requires continuous learning.

Direct with coaching

This point recognized that there are occasions when any manager or executive needs direction or guidance, especially when in an unfamiliar role or handling a new task beyond current capability. The 'with coaching' part reflected the approach required, when the leader was in a necessary control mode.

Delegate authority as well as responsibility

This was a particular issue with this culture, but occurs elsewhere and strikes at the heart of good leadership: knowing when to hand over the reins, as well as the horse!

Implications

Definition

Can we define leadership in a nutshell? I don't know about you, but if I had a leader who

■ was confident and capable

■ listened to me

■ supported me

- provided feedback and enabled me to grow and develop

- shared his or her thoughts, ideas and any other information with me

- was there to take the tough decisions, when needed

- provided guidance when I was uncertain and unsure, yet gave me the reins where I was confident and competent

I would be a very contented follower!

The benefits

Can good leadership be learned? Which of the above, whatever our current competence, can we not develop? We may not become perfect leaders, if there is such a thing, but we can all become good leaders, and reap the following benefits:

- It will improve the bottom-line.

- It will improve our self-image.

- It will improve the quality of our relationships.

- It will improve our career (however we define that).

And we can have a lot of fun on the way!

Leadership and development levels

We focused on leadership in the previous section, but, as already stated in the Introduction, as leaders we are also agents of change. If we become better leaders, we become better at initiating change. There is, inevitably, a strong link between change, development level and leadership, which we shall now explore.

Please refer back to Table 4.2. You will see that 'command and control' is the generic leadership approach we adopt when operating at security level. As we build our self-esteem, the need to control diminishes and our need to support increases. At the growth level, we use what I term 'questioning coach' at the individual level and 'visionary team' at the small group level. (The latter concept I first introduced in *The Power of Persuasion*, 1992.)

There is no single right answer to leadership or change management. There is, however, a direction and a desire.

Direction

To gain personal growth out of change, we must grow and develop our self-awareness, our self-esteem, our confidence and our competence. We cannot do that in isolation, but through interaction. We shall not gain personal growth unless we help others to gain personal growth.

While that is an overall direction, we also have to deal with the reality of ourselves and others. (In this chapter I focus on those we lead; in Chapter 6 I shall focus on those other individuals with whom we interact in our business lives.)

So, there needs to be a matching of leadership approaches to the people we lead. If we are happily grazing the green pastures of growth, and we are leading someone locked into the security level, we shall fail as leaders unless we recognize and react to that reality.

The reason why the individual is in security mode may be purely a function of 'personality', but is more likely to be because he or she is new to the job, or facing a complex task beyond current competence or meeting an 'impossible' deadline, or reacting to bad news (see the next chapter). Whatever the reasons, he or she will need a high degree of 'control' initially—being provided with a sense of direction and purpose to remove uncertainty.

Progressively, over time, we lessen the control and increase the support, which enables the 'follower' to build self-esteem. When both parties are operating at or near 'growth', the leader's role becomes 'questioning coach', which will often be, in fact, a shared voyage of discovery and learning, stretch and achievement. (The 'Visionary team' approach will be discussed in Chapter 8.)

Conversely, if we are temporarily or permanently at or near security level, we are bound to be poor leaders for those operating at levels higher than ours.

If we don't develop ourselves, we'll deny development to others.

Desire

If we examine the profile of the leader desired by managers and executives, it is not far from the 'questioning coach'. This reflects the reality that most of us are somewhere on the self-esteem level most of the time *and* we want and need to develop and grow. We seek the leadership style that satisfies our needs.

As followers, we want a 'questioning coach':

'What do you think our followers want?'

Whatever goals we set ourselves as leaders of change, we must always recognize the need to be flexible in the light of reality. While principle should drive experience, experience should also modify principle.

CASE
STUDY

On our Senior Executive Programme, Sir John Whitmore covers performance coaching. The executives are split into small groups of four or five. Each group has two land-skis—thin planks with holes equidistantly placed and with a rope running through each hole. The group assembles on the skis, with a rope in each hand, and a foot on each plank. The object of the exercise is to move to a marker, round it and back again as quickly as possible.

One person in each group is appointed leader/coach. As you can imagine, to start with it is a hilarious shambles. It takes an age to get to the marker, not too long to shuffle across and an age to get back.

However practice improves, and soon times get below 2 minutes. On one occasion, the three groups displayed considerable performance abilities quickly. So Sir John asked them to consider the 'turn'. They soon realized, after measuring relative times, that whereas the turn took very little time compared with the slow crawl forwards and backwards, it now took a disproportionately long time as compared to the fast walk backwards and forwards. The 'shuffle' could not be speeded up significantly.

Further debate and trials (just walking at the right pace) proved that the best turn of all was no turn at all! It was much faster to go past the marker and continue in a small arc and return on the other side without interrupting the rhythm.

Now something very interesting happened. Two groups accepted the new principle at the intellectual level only. They were not prepared to move away from the comfort levels established after so much uncertainty and discomfort, produced by the sudden change the outdoor environment and the initial exercise dictated.

The other group was prepared to have a go, as they were the more developed team! Initially, they fell on their faces—not in fact literally, but in terms of time taken.

Eventually, the two conservative groups, Sir John, and the cameraman (yours truly) watched and applauded the risk-taking group beat the all-comers record of 32 seconds!

There is another reality. After practice has improved performance with rules developed and the coach calling out the movements agreed, Sir John tells the groups to repeat the exercise with noone allowed to speak! Almost invariably, the groups go faster!

We shall explore some of the implications of this when looking at the skill of 'Promoting discovery' in Chapter 7.

The case study above was an example of the statement: '*principle should drive experience*', whereas the one below illustrates how '*experience should also modify principle*'.

CASE
STUDY

The personnel director of a profit-making organization was much taken with the 'empty vessel' versus 'acorn' view of management, and encouraged his managers to develop and apply coaching skills to promote discovery rather than give orders. He had a number of staff and adopted the same approach. One individual was very resistant and uncomfortable with the whole approach.

She basically wanted to be told what to do and had no desire to think for herself. The director persisted, but there was no change. He eventually gave up, disappointed, but recognizing that reality had to modify principle in this case.

Key point summary

- We operate in time and over time at different levels of development. Most individuals in employment vary from gaining *security* to developing *self-esteem* to achieving *growth*.

- The level at which we operate will determine how we react to change and whether we initiate change.

- Traumatic change pushes us down a level or two initially.

- Behaviours provide evidence of development level.

- Development level can be increased by reducing lower level behaviours, e.g. sarcasm, criticism, blaming, fault-finding and closed, judgemental questions and using growth behaviours like active listening, praising and open questioning.

- A pragmatic view of *leadership* is based on the views of the client or follower.

- There is a common core of thinking, which transcends status and culture.

- Requirements for good leaders are to:
  –think explicitly about the leadership role
  –develop self-awareness and self-belief
  –focus externally: listen, support, provide feedback and coach
  –display integrity in decision-taking and take decisions
  –share information
  –be confident enough to make mistakes, admit mistakes and learn from mistakes
  –direct with coaching
  –delegate authority as well as responsibility.

- The kind of leadership approach we adopt will depend on our development level, varying from 'command and control' to 'questioning coach' or 'visionary team'.

- Good leaders need to develop themselves before they can develop their followers. They are agents of change both for themselves and their followers.

- While the overall direction of leadership is towards 'questioning coach' or 'visionary team', there needs to be matching of leadership approach to the development level of the follower.

- Principle should drive experience, but, in the exception, principle needs to be altered by experience.

Your own points

Your action plan

Reacting to change

Introduction

In this chapter we look at the complete model of how we react to change (particularly sudden change), pulling together the themes and thoughts from the previous chapters. Initially, I concentrate on change that is perceived as highly significant such as job loss, sideways move, death of loved one and such events.

However, our lives are full of sudden little changes—the unexpected criticism, demand for work, new company edict and so on. So I also consider our reaction to such changes. For both categories, I look at how we can improve our response: reduce the negative and generate the positive.

Major sudden change

Before looking at the model, I share two examples of reacting to sudden, negative *personal* events, one much more traumatic than the other. This reinforces points already made in Chapter 3, and leads into the model. While transition and other curves abound in the literature, I have not come across one that links reaction to development level as explicitly as my model. However, there is nothing new under the sun and the model we look at could have been (in fact, was) developed from practice rather than theory: it emanated from all the individual responses to the change preference assessment.

Jean

The event: Death of a parent.

Q1—Prior to the event: I was told accidentally by another child. Although I knew that something was not right, no one had told me of my father's death.

Q2—Source of information and feeling: Anger, disbelief and grief. Anger at the child, and anger towards my mother for not having told me.

Q3–What the change involved: I had little sense of the change involved, partly because adults tried to shield me from it. A pretence at normality actually did not hide from me the fact that there was a change. It also seemed a denial of my ability even as a child to recognize the enormity of the change that was impacting on me.

Q4–Your views considered: I was not consulted as to my beliefs, feelings–the assumptions were made as to what was going to be right for me. From my mother's perspective, this was 'pretending everything was as it was before, and let us not talk about things'.

Q5–The lead up and change in attitude: Even as child (of 7), I knew that things were going on around me that I was being excluded from. I felt out of control, while I saw that other people (and even other children) had more information than I had. The change (in attitude) I remember is a feeling of distrust and contempt for adults, who believed they could make things OK for me by giving me presents. This was probably the first time I saw adults as failing me.

Q6–During the event: I could not have anticipated the event, as it came as a complete bombshell. My thoughts were ones of disbelief, anger and overwhelming sadness.

Q7–After the event: I think the episode made me ill-equipped to deal with change, and developed in me a tendency to avoid recognizing things I can sense as happening around me, because of enormous fear that in verbalizing issues something dreadful will happen. It also made me see myself as a unit that is safer when self-contained, so that I can deal with issues at the pace I choose, rather than having them thrown at me.

Q8–Advice on learning from change: My learnings have been that everyone regardless of age has the ability to deal with change more positively if:

- they are treated with respect as an equal and assumptions about their needs, and coping abilities are not made by others;

- they are allowed to express feelings and ideas, rather than being constrained as to what is OK and not OK to express;

- they are consulted as to what is right for them;

- the nature of change is made visible to them.

These are powerful, positive comments, to which we shall return in the next chapter when we look further at how you can help others gain personal growth out of change.

It is no surprise that Jean's profile is strongly PF/PC, reflecting the learning.

Jean's profile:

LD	NC	PF	PC
25	20	**38**	**37**

I do not necessarily know all the respondents to the questionnaire, but I have met Jean. She is a rare individual, who operates most of the time near the growth level.

Funnily enough, she does not recognize this, and has a humility and perceived inadequacy in reacting to or initiating change, which belies her actual competence and capability. She practises what she prefers, when it comes to change.

I would also imagine that she had developed an inner core of strength by the time she was 7—if this event represented the first time adults had let her down.

Before moving on, I would emphasize the emotional reaction: *'anger, disbelief and grief'*.

Debbie

The event: Sexual assault—rape.

Q1—Prior to the event: As an assault it was sudden.

Q2—Source of information and feeling: The immediate reaction was one of 'this is not happening to me'. Shock, I suppose.

Q3—What the change involved: Immediate reaction was one of knowing 'nobody can come near me'. Did not realize how long this would last and still have a very strong sense of my own personal space. I can also get upset very easily if someone—even someone I know well—invades this space suddenly. I certainly did not realize for a long time why I reacted the way I did. The full effect on me came out over a period of time.

Q4—Your views considered: Comfort offered by some, but not understood by most. I did not generally talk of this and it was probably a period of 6-8 years before I mentioned it to more than three or four people. The boyfriend at the time laughed— he obviously couldn't cope with it himself, but didn't want to know how I felt. (The relationship quite quickly came to an end afterwards although we had been going out for approx 18 months—brute!!)

Q5—The lead up and change in attitude:

- Hadn't really thought about it before—not the sort of thing that happens to you.

- I've never been a particularly tactile person, but less so since the incident.

- I am very cautious, and aware of potentially dangerous situations, which others do not see.

Q7—After the event: The negative emotional response can still easily come to the surface through throwaway comments, e.g. 'if you are going to be raped, you might as well enjoy it', makes me exceptionally angry, or 'Rape—as if you would be so lucky'.

Q8—Advice on learning from change: Probably seek professional counselling in order to express/release feelings asap. With me, it certainly had a detrimental effect on my relationships with the opposite sex.

Debbie's profile:

LD	NC	PF	PC
37	35	24	24

Traumatic, negative change inevitably means that we take a hit, move down a development level, become cautious or wary and need to control. Sometimes change towards a more flexible and open approach takes a long time. That too must be explicitly recognized.

Reaction through to growth

Now let us turn to the model. Would you please study Figure 5.1. Personal growth is the ultimate prize, but by the very nature of the change experienced this can be difficult to reach and, as we have said, takes time.

I shall explain the chart in some detail. We are looking at how we react to sudden negative change, the phases of reaction we go through over time, and the impact those phases have on our development level. The assumption in Figure 5.1 is that we are fairly high on the self-esteem level— we have quite a strong belief in our self-worth, our competence and our capability. If you like, we are quite mature.

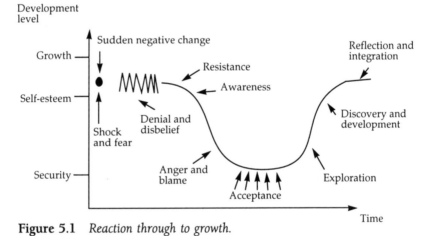

Figure 5.1 *Reaction through to growth.*

Shock and denial

The first reaction is one of shock. As mentioned in earlier chapters, the suddenness, coupled with the lack of continuity, means that there is no connection with our existing mental model of reality. We have had no prior warning nor expectation of the event. Our reaction is purely instinctive and 'animal'. We are caught like a rabbit in the sudden glare of the headlights of a car, and freeze.

We do not believe what we necessarily cannot believe—we deny the actuality that, at that moment in time, has no meaning.

This is usually a short-lived phase, but not necessarily so. The key factors at play are:

- the nature of the sudden change

- the degree of evidence, supporting the new change

- our development level.

Looking at the latter factor first, I would draw your attention to Figure 5.2 entitled 'Dichotomy'. This represents someone who is immature and operating at the security level—a child.

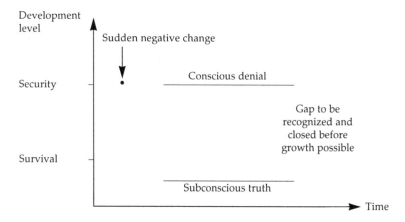

Figure 5.2 *Dichotomy.*

What happens is that the denial phase becomes permanent, because acceptance threatens survival—the basic level. We have all read about or seen films where children have been exposed to some traumatic event, which has been locked into the subconscious and denied at the conscious level. This dichotomy is carried into adulthood, but until the wound is revealed so that it can be cleansed and the healing process begun, growth is impossible because the adult-child spends her or his time searching for answers to a question that is unknown.

We have come across this dichotomy before, when criticism is coming from the security rather than the self-esteem level. The pattern can be picked up if the fault being criticized is not person specific but fault specific.

Some people use the word hypocrisy–criticizing in others what we fail to see in ourselves. Maybe we would change our attitude if we realized that 'hypocrisy' demonstrates a high, but unrecognized and unfulfilled, need for security.

Most adults first deny and then begin the process of acceptance, assisted by evidence, be it P45 or the body of a loved one who has died. Evidence is crucial to acceptance, whether it is physical evidence or the word of someone we trust–a point to bear in mind when we initiate change for others.

The absence of a body increases the probability of denial of death. Even if we have evidence, because it is a physical event like rape, then the blame and the shame and the loss of self-esteem can lead to conscious rejection, and to the dichotomy of the child. This is likely if that trauma occurred when the individual was already at a low level.

Resistance and awareness

However, assuming that we move beyond denial, then we will resist the dawning of the new, unpleasant reality. We are starting a process of integrating the new with the old, and initially we have to resist so that we can close the gap slowly. It is important, where we are responsible for the shock, that we understand this and have all the evidence at our disposal to overcome this inevitable resistance.

Sometimes we can be too logical and emotional: 'Don't you believe me? I wouldn't lie to you. Are you calling me a liar?', and so on.

Resistance is also inevitable, because we are subconsciously fighting the descent down a development level. When we are sacked, we lose self-esteem, we lose confidence, and our competence declines. We become more insecure. Few seek out that reality.

CASE STUDY

A professional was made redundant during the recession. She was very competent, but the organization had decided that, because of cost-cutting necessitated by the recession, her function was no longer required. She was clearly advised of this, but for some time felt that she was incompetent.

Evidence played a strong part in overcoming that perception, as the organization subsequently used her services as an independent, and paid her roughly twice the amount she received when salaried!

Anger and blame

As we become more aware that this change represents a new reality and as our resistance is overcome, we stay gripped by emotion. The emotion associated with shock is fear, an inevitable consequence of the high level of uncertainty instantly generated. Now, the emotion is one of anger and blame. We 'kick against the pricks', 'rail against fate'.

The anger can be both internally and externally focused.

- The higher our self-esteem, the less anger there is, and the more it is externally focused.

- The lower our development level, the more anger there is and the more internally focused it becomes over time.

Part of self-blame that can linger into and beyond acceptance is regret: 'If only, I had …'. How often do children blame themselves, their perceived incompetence and inadequacy, for their parents' divorce? How often does regret for the passing of good times stay with us for ever?

On a lighter note, I find it fascinating that writing about change helps me to become more observant. A case in point:

While I was writing this chapter, my son Edward brought a school-mate Peter home for supper. I was introduced, and they were playing while I was writing. There was a crash, then a cry. Peter had fallen down our slippery stairs and hurt his back—a sudden negative shock.

Tears ensued (disbelief would have been very temporary as this was a highly physical event). Comfort and support was critical, a detailed examination of the wound-free area and so on. What was interesting was the debate. While Peter had been warned about the stairs, he was a very confident extrovert with very low listening skills. Suddenly Edward, in the eyes of Peter, became the villain of the piece—the cause of the accident, although he was blameless. The debate continued for a while, and then, as often the case, pain and memory receded and all was forgotten.

CASE STUDY

Even with this minor event, the emotion and the need to blame was there.

- Confident extroverts tend to blame others—and get the balance wrong.

- Less confident introverts tend to blame themselves—and get the balance wrong.

Blame is a necessary, but fundamentally counter-productive phase, associated with the emotional response.

If we are operating at a high development level, then the blame phase tends to be temporary and not too intense.

This a fundamental point in relation to the curve on Figure 5.1. The higher our existing self-esteem the quicker the transition and the shallower the dip in terms of loss of confidence and self-esteem. There is unfortunately an element of the virtuous and the vicious in our reactions to sudden negative change. The lower our self-esteem, the more vicious the reaction and the higher the more virtuous.

Acceptance

So, most of us will move eventually–it may be hours, days, weeks, months or even years–to acceptance. However, the nature of that acceptance and the extent to which it is a temporary phase on a downward or upward path will vary. In explaining this, may I draw your attention to the lower part of Figure 5.1 where acceptance of the negative change can be seen to be a low point in terms of self-esteem/development level.

In the downward phase, we tend to be emotional, supported by irrational and negative logic, and very internally focused. We have taken a hit, and we tend to look within to heal. Our inner world expands. In fact we can become locked into that world, and in danger of locking out our external environment to the extent of being swallowed by our excessive introversion.

Recognition of the likely reaction curve is critically important, as it enables us to move from unconscious incompetence (at the mercy of winds of reaction that we do not recognize) to conscious incompetence (knowing what emotions are gripping us and why; which makes it possible for our cerebral side to intervene positively).

What we need to do is force ourselves to bring into the dark side a little, at least, of the light of rational and positive thinking.

We have to use our intellect to break out of introversion. If we can do this, whatever our starting point, we change the nature of the acceptance– less blame and less pain, more balanced and more positive. We have already sown the seeds of growth as we are geared up to move more swiftly into, and higher up, the growth phase. There is a necessity to deliberately seek external stimulus to compensate for the internal and negative reaction. That external stimuli should include emotional support. We need to touch the hand that is outstretched or seek a hand to touch, even though it goes against the grain.

EXAMPLE My wife works at a nursery, where there is a woman with grown-up children. Her husband, to whom she was very close, died suddenly, and the natural temptation was to withdraw into herself and become dependent on her children. She recognized the danger, and, as an example, forced herself to go abroad on holiday on her own. She was very reluctant, frightened and uncertain. She made new friends, discovered that she could cope on her own, and now has an independent life which is fulfilling and which she treasures.

Exploration, discovery and integration

Provided the nature of our acceptance has a rational and positive dimension, then we shall move into exploration. We have to fight to be rational, to accentuate the positive we do not feel, to seek support, to retain balance, to force out blame and replace it with detached understanding, thereby preserving as much self-esteem as we can. We must let the heart weep (mourning is vital) but force the head to change the heart.

You may have noticed that many of the respondents to the questionnaire highlighted the need to 'trust your instincts'. This was a point debated at some length among a group of managers at one point. The view, which was a consensus, was that if we genuinely listened, explored and evaluated alternatives and options, the very process meant that when we tapped into our gut feeling, it had actually changed from the original emotional or instinctive response.

We are complex creatures. Often we are driven by emotions, and use irrational logic to justify them. We tend to feel before we think. However, if we are prepared to listen, to explore—to open up and open out—then the emotion and the intuition will change. Intuition, after all, is the subconscious learning from experience. If we are prepared to expose ourselves to new thoughts, new feelings and new experiences, our learning and intuition will change.

So the key to the ascent up the growth phase is to explore and evaluate (PC and LD) from the base of acceptance—not, however, on our own, but with others (PF)—to discover new meaning and to develop new skills to use those hidden strengths, which adversity brings closer to the surface. They are strengths that we concsciously need to uncover and tap into.

Finally, we need to integrate the new learning with the past, which was so suddenly changed. We need to review and reflect—to look back not in anger, but with understanding.

This is one reason why I asked you to fill in the questionnaire on an important experience of change. If you did not choose a sudden, negative change, then perhaps you feel comfortable with doing so now. Even if you did, it is worth revisiting the change or selecting a different experience. It will help with your own learning if you do so, and also help you help others. The questions are different, and are set out below:

Q1.   What was the exact nature of the event or change?

Q2.   Did you have any inkling or were you prepared for it in any way?

Q3. How did you find out?

Q4. What was your immediate reaction—how did you feel, and what did you say and do?

Q5. For how long were you in the grip of emotion, and what did you do to release the emotional tensions?

Q6. Who did you blame? Did you blame yourself? Do you still carry feelings of anger and blame?

Q7. How long was it before you fully accepted the change, and what steps did you take to uncover positive aspects?

Q8. To what extent did you ask for and receive or be offered and accept comfort and emotional support?

Q9. Have you moved beyond acceptance into exploration, discovery and integration of learning? Have you completed the transition, and, if not, what are you going to do to ensure real personal growth?

Q10. If you were to have a similar experience, what would you do differently and why?

The power of language

Before we move on to the second section of this chapter—reacting to minor sudden change—it is important to recognize the role played by language. We tend to use words that reinforce the negative and explicitly reduce our self-esteem, or others do so in describing the negative event we are experiencing. This is counter-productive, and we should deliberately use language that is neutral or positively descriptive. What we say affects the way we feel. Language is very important.

'We are letting you go' is better than 'you are sacked', and certainly better than 'we are giving you your freedom!' On the other side of the coin 'I've lost my job'—a statement of fact—is far better than 'I've been sacked', where we verbally confirm our perception of our own incompetence. A change to be managed is better than a problem to be solved. 'My relationship with Paul is over' is better than 'Paul dumped me' or 'I dumped Paul'.

Perceptions will change if we deliberately use the correct language.

Reacting to minor sudden change

As mentioned in the beginning of this chapter, our daily lives are full of little sudden changes, both positive and negative. There is always potential for effective response to such changes, but often we respond explicitly or implicitly instantly and emotionally, and fail to achieve the growth that is there—both for us and for others.

Some examples of such sudden little changes are:

- criticism or praise
- request from our boss
- being presented with a *fait accompli*, e.g. edict from our company, reducing benefits or introducing some new rule which affects us
- being imposed upon: 'Could you run off 30 photocopies for me?'
- a proposal or idea from a 'subordinate'
- interruptions.

Now there is a very simple way of achieving growth from such changes. It is simple for me to say, but difficult to do. *Be truly assertive.* A truly assertive response combines the LD/PC and PF modes, which, as we have discovered, are the modes to generate growth for ourselves and others.

As this is such an important area, where unfortunately there is much misconception and malpractice, I shall devote some time to it. The objective is for you to be confident in your ability to use practical approaches to generate growth outcomes, when the changes are sudden but not very significant. If changes are sudden or significant and are perceived inevitably (in the initial emotional reaction) as negative, there is bound to be a downward spiral.

If the changes are small in dimension, then we can fairly easily and instantly eradicate the small downward potential with the application of technique, and then go for growth.

As an aside, it still surprises me just how often the word assertive is used, not just in training circles but by individuals. A few months ago I was running a Senior Executive Programme and out of the ten delegates, four expressed the need to be more assertive as a priority development need. Two were coming from the reality of being too aggressive, and two from being submissive.

In looking at assertiveness, I shall consider misconception, meaning, examples and technique.

Misconception

Misconception as to what constitutes assertive behaviour arises for two reasons: limitation or development.

Limitations of language

The dictionary, as one would expect, defines assertion as 'insistence on a right or opinion'—a rather aggressive definition! From this, comes the view of assertiveness as asserting your rights in a non-aggressive way. But this is one-way traffic. True assertiveness or effective assertive behaviour is a mutuality concept, not an individual ego concept.

If one reads practitioners, you see movement away from the ego base. Here are three definitions:

■ 'The positive, honest statement of our feelings, wants or desires of other people, expressed in a balanced way.'

■ 'Standing up for our own rights in a way that does not violate another person's rights.'

■ 'Expressing oneself in such a way as to achieve and maintain the right balance between one's own rights and obligations and the rights and obligations of others.'

What is the right balance? Are we more attracted to our rights or our obligations or responsibilities?

Development level

As we have already seen, because of upbringing and circumstance, we can vary from being locked into a lower development level such as survival or security, or be operating in the main at a higher level such as self-esteem or growth. Within that overall context, in the course of events during a day, we may well move between levels, reacting to criticism at one moment and moving to security, enjoying an effective dialogue with a colleague, both at growth level, or focusing on completing a task—building our self-esteem.

Most of us don't operate at growth level very often, and so there is a bias in the teaching and understanding of assertiveness, from self-defence classes (security) to asserting rights, but recognizing responsibilities (self-esteem).

Meaning

Assertiveness is a mutuality concept. When we are assertive we are operating at the highest level—the growth level. *To be effective, we must bring the person with whom we are interacting to the same level.* We are assertive, when we behave in a way that gives effective expression to the rights of both parties involved. So we need to be proactive, though we are reacting, and we need to understand the other party's feelings and point of view if our response is to be effective.

The fundamental basis for assertive behaviour is mutual respect. If we do not truly respect ourselves, have self-esteem, then we shall be aggressive or submissive. If our lack of self-respect is a subconscious reality, we are likely to be aggressive. If it is a conscious reality, we are likely to be submissive. If we respect only ourselves and not others, we are likely to be aggressive.

Now, if we have low self-esteem, you might wonder how we can possibly be effectively assertive. That is the beauty of technique, based on a sound principle. If we can follow a simple technique which produces effective outcomes, then the lack of self-esteem does not matter. Success repeated over time changes the belief.

Examples

These examples are taken from a video produced by my former colleague Vered Dinour.

Handling poor criticism (1)

AGGRESSIVELY

John (Boss): Ah! Graham. Thanks for all the hard work you've put into this campaign, but as you know it's been going on for two months now, and the results are absolutely dreadful. Quite frankly I can't afford to carry deadweight anymore.

Graham: I think I'm the best judge of results in this particular case, seeing as how you haven't shown any interest up to today.

Fighting fire with fire is rarely a good strategy generally, and particularly if you are a subordinate!

ASSERTIVELY

John: Ah! Graham. Thanks for all the hard work you've put into this campaign, but as you know it's been going on for two months now, and the results are absolutely dreadful. Quite frankly I can't afford to carry deadweight anymore.

Graham: John—I can hear what you say, and understand what you say. I know the campaign wasn't as good as we hoped it would be, but as you say I have put a lot of hard work into it, and I would like us to spend some time going over the campaign to see how I managed it and to see what good points there were in it, and what we can learn from it.

John: I think we should—as soon as possible.

Graham: Fine, I'll arrange a time later on today.

John: I look forward to it.

There were four key positive features to Graham's approach:

- Refusal to respond to the personal attack, the feature of the aggressive response.

- Accepting what was valid in the criticism undefensively.

- Seeing criticism as an opportunity to improve future performance rather than to harp on past failure.

- Refusing to become a scapegoat, through inviting John into a joint problem-solving discussion.

Handling poor criticism (2)

AGGRESSIVELY

Boss (on phone): See you at the usual 9 o'clock tee-off. Bye. (*Puts phone down and turns to colleague.*) John—why haven't we done something about the Morrison account? I was at the Institute's dinner last night when the MD pulled me aside, complained bitterly about the slow service and wants action now.

John: They'll just have to wait; we're absolutely snowed under.

Boss: They won't just have to wait. I want something done today.

John: Fine. If that's an order. But if we get into any difficulties in our major account as a result, I'm putting them straight through to you.

ASSERTIVELY

Boss (on phone): See you at the usual 9 o'clock tee-off. Bye. (*Puts phone down and turns to colleague.*) John—why haven't we done something about the Morrison account? I was at the Institute's dinner last night when the MD pulled me aside, complained bitterly about the slow service and wants action now.

John: That must have been very embarrassing for you. I wouldn't have liked to be in your shoes.

Boss: It was John. I want something done today.

John: I see. Let's agree to work to our basic strategy. Morrisons are not one of our biggest accounts, very important though they are. We're snowed under, doing the Smith project that we've got to deliver on Friday. We've got no capacity this week. We could look at organizing our priorities for next week though, and that would help them.

Boss: Well, what do you expect me to tell Morrison?

John: Well, why don't you tell them that as a result of the conversation you had last week, you've looked at the production schedule. His will be the next project that we take on board, and we'll confirm the proposal by hand next Wednesday.

Boss: OK John, that'll do, that'll do.

This demonstrates the key features of an assertive response:

- Both parties started from the same point, i.e. they are both angry at having failed to meet customer expectations. The instant reaction is to blame (boss) and reject criticism (John), as happened in the first scenario. The difference develops from John's recognition of his boss's position, evidenced by his empathetic comment. He suppresses the instant negative or NC response, and moves into PF.

- After recognizing and reacting positively to the emotional base to this discussion, John moved forward by using facts (LD) rather than displaying his own feelings (NC).

- Using PC, John looks to a solution that takes care of the needs of all parties rather than one that leaves winners and losers (LD/NC).

Receiving praise

Carol: Hi Robert. I was most impressed by that software you designed. It's
very original and works well. The client was delighted.

Robert: It was nothing *or* It's hardly original *or* Well most of the ideas were
yours, I just put them together really.

In rejecting the praise, Robert is undervaluing his skill. If he was prepared
to accept the judgement of his boss, he would begin to develop greater
appreciation of his own worth, helping both his confidence and
competence. Additionally, he is rejecting the giver and her judgement–
praise is less likely to be forthcoming in the future. The final version adds
an attempt at flattery, encouraging a wrong motivation for the future use of
praise, if Carol is susceptible, as she might be.

The assertive response is simply 'Thank you' or 'Thank you. It's nice to
know it's appreciated.' In accepting the gift of praise, he is accepting the
giver.

There is a general perception that there is too much criticism and too
little praise in organizations, despite the need for recognition when we are
developing our self-esteem. One reason is that many of us are bad at
accepting praise, and so it becomes a rarity.

The assertive deputy?

The background to the exchange is that the head of department (Paul)
doesn't like doing staff appraisals, as he finds them difficult. The senior
manager Charles, to whom he talks, is aware of this, although it has never
been explicitly agreed. The first result comes from the effective use of
flattery by Paul.

Paul: You know I have Liam's appraisal to do tomorrow. Well, I can't do it,
because I have to see a client. There's no one else I can ask to do it for
me, because I know it's going to be a rather difficult interview. I think
you are the only person I could trust to deal with it. I've been very
impressed by the way you've dealt with things in the past. You won't let
me down, will you?

Charles: Well thank you. Yes I think I could probably do that. By the way,
where are you meeting the client?

Paul: Well actually, it's on the golf course!

(Notice how the redundant 'actually' invariably hides some discomfort,
not being expressed.)

At this juncture, Charles decides to be assertive. Write down what you
would say to Paul as Charles.

CHARLES'S FOLLOW-UP

Now compare this assertive response with your own written suggestion.

Charles: Well actually I've got something else arranged and, more importantly, I think you should consider whether a social meeting with a client should take priority over an appraisal meeting with your staff.

I'll bet your suggestion was better. The response above belongs to the aggressive school of assertion. It is certainly effective in asserting George's right to say no, but it does not belong to the mutuality school, nor for that matter to the career progressive school!

Bosses do not take kindly, in my experience, to being told off by a subordinate. This is why people schooled in the non-aggressive view of assertion find it less than successful when putting it into practice.

In my view, the key to the answer is for Charles to say no, as is his right, but to recognize the right of his boss not to be comfortable with appraisals. Paul has probably deliberately arranged his golf game to coincide with the appraisal and appointed Charles as someone who doesn't say no.

With the response as stated, we have the classic situation of the worm turning—straight from submissiveness to aggression, masking as assertiveness.

Maybe something along these lines:

Charles: I'm sorry. I've remembered that I'm doing an appraisal myself! Tell you what. Why don't you fix a time with Liam you can make, and, as he has worked for me, we could have a chat about his performance and the problems he poses before you see him?

Note: White lies are an excellent tool to improve change and time management!

Techniques

The assertive pause

We have seen examples of assertive and proactive responses to emotional and potentially negative situations, which are quite frequent in their occurrence.

The secret is to control our own knee-jerk reactions—to avoid the instant NC. This is not possible with significant change in the instant of impact, though we should implement a deliberate strategy of limiting the downward spiral of NC (supported by irrational logic) through conscious efforts to gain support, to rationalize and to explore beyond the boundaries we currently perceive.

This is all very well, but how do we do it? Well, there is no magic, we simply train ourselves to pause before we react. I call it the assertive pause. It is not just any old pause. We deliberately breathe deeply—what the experts call 'breathing through the rib cage'. Usually we breathe shallowly at the top of our chest or throat. In fact, sudden stress can produce an exaggeration of this normal mode—hyperventilation.

Incidentally, this is why aerobic exercises like jogging, swimming or cycling are so good for us, because we breathe through the rib cage when performing these exercises. We breathe shallowly when playing squash, because of the pace. Yet so many people use squash to try to release tension!

From a physiological perspective, by breathing deeply, we take much more oxygen into our lungs than usual, which is transmitted to our brains. We literally 'clear our minds'. This enables us to eradicate the instant negative emotional response and to move into LD (facts) and PC (options) before taking a decision. It enables us to be assertive.

EXAMPLE

I was talking to a manager about work allocations among secretaries, and he passed on what he thought was sound advice, given to him by a senior man many years earlier. He put a problem to me. 'You have, say, a proposal to get typed urgently. Your secretary is absent. What would you do?', he asked me. I replied, 'Well, if I did not have time to type it myself, I would find a secretary who was not too busy and ask her to do it.' 'Wrong,' he said, 'totally wrong, my boy. You find the secretary who is always very busy, and give it to her.'

As you will appreciate, his logic was simple. The idle secretaries had learned the art of saying no (to excess) and the busy ones had not. Also, the busy ones were competent and the idle ones less so. It is sad, but true, and is not limited to secretaries!

Continuing the description of the *assertive pause* technique, once we have cleared our minds we can move into rational LD and PC, before coming to a decision that is acceptable to the other party. Take, as an example, a secretary who is subject to a sudden request to do extra work, and usually responds with the bald non-assertive 'yes' or the bald aggressive 'no'.

Harriet: Jane, Graham needs a proposal typing urgently. You are the only one available. So, could you please do it?

Jane: (ASSERTIVE PAUSE) When is the exact deadline, Harriet?

Harriet: Graham says he needs it by 5 o'clock.

Jane: Well, I'm very busy today, with two proposals to be completed and, as they take over an hour, I haven't the time today. I have a less busy schedule tomorrow—so I could help out, if the deadline became tomorrow. OK?

Harriet: Fair enough. Thanks.

Jane retains control in an assertive way. If the deadline is genuine she does not do the extra work. If the deadline is changed she will do the work, as she now has the time to do it and can plan it in advance into her schedule. She also avoids perjorative labels of 'push-over' or 'skiver'.

Key point summary

■ There is a clear reaction curve when we are faced with sudden change, perceived negatively.

■ The instant reaction is one of disbelief, because the event does not connect with our model of reality. If the change is highly traumatic, or if we are operating at a low development level, disbelief or rejection can become permanent at the conscious level.

■ If we are initiating change, and circumstances force us to make the announcement suddenly or less gradually than we would prefer, we should ensure that we have all tangible evidence available to help overcome the rejection phase.

■ If we are mature—operating at a high development level—or the change is sudden but not too traumatic and has been evidenced, we shall move into negative emotional response. We shall descend down to self-esteem or into security, inevitably losing confidence as well as self-esteem.

■ We shall be angry with ourselves for letting the event take place, and be angry with those causing it. We shall start criticizing and blaming self and the other(s).

■ The lower our initial development level, the more intense and self-centred our negative emotional response, the steeper and further the descent, and the more blame we heap on ourselves.

■ As we move to acceptance, emotional intensity diminishes, though feelings of regret and sadness linger on.

■ We need to recognize the inevitability of the reaction curve, and the need to force ourselves to think rationally, seek support and focus externally. This will reduce the depth and length of the negative phase and optimize our ability to take advantage of the growth phase.

■ There is a powerful pull towards an 'instinctive' or 'gut feel' response. We should delay making decisions until we have achieved an external focus, as that will improve our instinctive response, and increase growth.

■ Where change is sudden, but not significant, we can minimize or avoid the negative reaction by focusing on assertive responses.

■ We need to recognize the principle of mutuality underpinning growth-level assertiveness, and use the *assertive pause* technique to release tension, control our negative emotional reaction, and enable us to explore options and implications that lead to a decision that is acceptable to both parties.

Your own points

Initiating change

Introduction

In this chapter, we look at how we initiate change. There are a number of possibilities to be considered.

- *Initiating change for ourselves*   This could be any change in our business or personal circumstances, where we are proactive—we seek what we consider will help us. In business terms, it could vary from deciding we wanted to change the nature of our work with our existing employer to deciding to change employers.

- *Initiating change in ourselves*   We have identified a strength we want to develop or a weakness we want to overcome—we have climbed the learning ladder out of unconscious incompetence in some area and want to progress.

- *Initiating change in others*   We want to persuade someone to change—to become different or do something different, as that will benefit us or that person, or both parties.

- *Initiating change through others*   This can occur when we are in reaction or initiation mode.

Reaction

Business examples would be:

- As the MD of a subsidiary, set demanding profitability targets by the main board. This often happens! The achievement of that will be down to others.

- A new performance appraisal is being introduced, where there has been little or no consultation with section heads. As section heads, we shall not only need to use it ourselves on our subordinate managers, but ensure that they downstream this change effectively as well as perform effectively in carrying out appraisals of their subordinates.

■ Project leaders of a new project.

Initiation

Whenever we have a role of 'managing through others', we can initiate changes within our discretion that others will implement.

'Change involving others' is not a separate category, as almost all change we initiate will involve others. That is an aspect running through this chapter.

The last category, 'initiating change through others', is only looked at on an individual rather than a team or organizational basis, as these are covered in the chapters on 'Growing the team' and 'Growing the organization'.

'Initiating change in ourselves' has already been covered, as has, to some extent, 'initiating change for ourselves'.

So the focus of this chapter is how we influence or persuade others on an individual basis to do something we want them to do, or to make a change we want them to make. At the end we shall also consider the model we can develop on initiating a change for ourselves.

Persuading others to change

Some of the material in this section is based on my book *The Power of Persuasion: Improving your Performance and Leadership Skills*. There is also new material.

As mentioned in the Preface, this chapter provides you with the opportunity to determine your own profile before asking a colleague, preferably someone who reports directly to you, to fill in the questionnaire in the appendix. The reasons a 'subordinate' is suggested are:

■ It is with followers that perception gaps most often arise.

■ We have the greatest ability to help followers gain growth out of change through the quality of our leadership.

■ Followers produce results for which we are held accountable by our own bosses.

After that has been completed, you can compare her or his view of how you persuade with your own views and consider the strengths and any gaps in perception. As also mentioned in the Preface, you have an opportunity, best seized when you have read the next chapter, to put theory into practice—to change the quality of a business relationship for the better and enable both yourself and the other person to gain personal growth as a result.

However, before involving anyone else, we shall describe the four different approaches.

The four persuasion approaches

The definitions of the four approaches can be seen in Table 6.1. To develop understanding, let us take an example of a specific situation where a manager, Helen, is talking to a subordinate, George, about his performance against targets during the year. It is part of the annual appraisal.

Table 6.1 The four persuasion approaches

I = Incentives	L = Logic	E = Empathy	G = Group
Incitement to action through the use of one or more of: ■ Financial rewards ■ Non-financial rewards ■ Praise ■ Flattery ■ Threats (open and veiled) ■ Criticism	Correct or incorrect use of the intellectual faculty whereby conclusions are drawn through connecting facts (or opinions serving as facts) in a structured way	The power of entering into the feeling and spirit of another person and so appreciating her or him fully	The creation or use of a common understanding of a shared vision

Helen: Let's recap. You have exceeded your target of chargeable hours completed in the year, and you have met the target of 12 proposals for new business. That's excellent work, George. Well done.

George: Thank you.

Helen: However, you have failed to meet your other main target. You were supposed to bring in £200 000 new business and have only managed £120 000—a significant shortfall of £80 000. According to my notes, the shortfall at the half-year was only £10 000. What went wrong?

George: We missed the big sale to Wentworth by a whisker. There were only ourselves and Cordles in the frame, and they went for Cordles on price, acknowledging that they thought our quality would be better. That cost us £90 000 and if we had got it, I would have exceeded my sales target.

Helen: That must have a big blow for you, getting so close and then losing out.

George: It was, and it's blown my figures for this year. But all is not lost. We are down to the final beauty parade with Comsac. I am leading the team presentation, and it is worth over 150k if we win.

Helen: That is excellent news, indeed. I'll keep my fingers crossed for you. Can I help at all?

George: Thanks. Actually, you can. It's your area of expertise. Could you glance over the draft slides for the presentation and let me know of any improvements you think I should make, before I call a team meeting?

Helen: Of course, we need to pull together as a team if we are going to win in the marketplace. As regards your overall grading, I think you have done very well this year. You have shown a lot of commitment, energy and put in good work. Given the circumstances of the lost sale, and the fact that it has been tough this year, so few of your peers have met their targets, I suggest an overall grade of 4–above average performance. Are you happy with that?

George: Yes, that's very fair and much appreciated.

Helen: Good. That's settled. Let us look at your development plan for next year. ...

Incentives

We use the 'stick' and the 'carrot' to encourage desired behaviour, to motivate people to perform and sometimes, when supported by positional power, to persuade them to do what we think is best for them!

When we praise or blame, we are in the incentive persuasion mode. If we are feeling insecure, we shall often use the negative side to try to control others. If we are at a higher level of development, we shall use the positive side to encourage and support others.

As is often the case, the way we say things will determine whether we are seen as using negative 'incentives' or rational 'logic'.

Helen uses incentives positively: 'That's excellent work'; 'That's excellent news, indeed'. She also said 'you have failed to meet your other main target'. If that was said calmly and dispassionately, it would indicate the use of rational logic. If an edge crept into the voice, it would be perceived by George as critical.

When using incentives, we are often driven by our own emotions, which, as we have seen, can be dressed up in logic.

Logic

Logic is used to develop knowledge, decide rationally and, sometimes, to win arguments, using the 'incorrect use of reasoning' or prejudicial approach.

Helen was mainly in the logical persuasion mode, using the facts and asking questions to uncover answers.

Empathy

With empathy, we display good questioning and listening skills, and supporting body language. It is very powerful as we effectively communicate to other people the message that we care for them, we understand them and we know and appreciate their point of view. We are explicitly (in the eyes of the other person we are persuading) acknowledging their value and importance as human beings and individuals. We all respond to such an approach.

Sometimes, when using the empathy persuasion mode, we may be seen as manipulative (exposing others and not ourselves) or non-assertive—falling over to please.

Helen displayed a fair degree of empathy—listening and adjusting in the light of information received: 'That must have been a big blow for you'; 'I'll keep my fingers crossed for you'.

Group

This is the persuasion mode of vision and ideas, trying to generate or develop a group or team spirit. The approach can be used at any level—international, national, company and team—and can be very powerful as we all dream dreams and can be inspired by the visionary.

Helen made some use of group persuasion: 'We need to pull together as a team if we are going to win in the marketplace.'

If, from this scenario, I were to guess Helen's profile, I would give a fairly high logic and empathy score (the assertive persuasion combination), moderate group and low incentives.

Her profile is shown in Figure 6.1.

Assessing yourself

You will notice on Figure 6.2 that 20 points have been allocated to each persuasion approach. You might well feel that this represents spurious accuracy, when you are being asked purely to estimate.

■ First of all, a numbered system helps you to differentiate between strong, moderate or weak use of a particular approach when making your decision.

■ Secondly, the questionnaire your colleague completes is detailed, and so you will be able to produce an accurate profile of his or her perception.

■ Thirdly, when interpreting the results, a gap of a few points is not significant, and so your approximation does not matter.

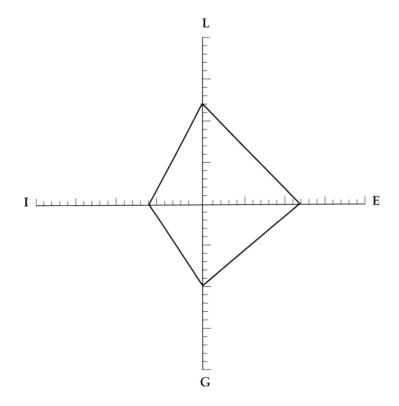

Figure 6.1 *Helen's profile.*

Now the way we persuade people to make a change we want them to make can vary according to the level of the relationship, the nature of the relationship, and the specific situation, e.g. how comfortable we feel.

This is why it is sensible to identify a specific individual, think of your relationship with that person, and cast your mind back to specific situations where you have tried to persuade him or her to do something. Having reflected on that, estimate the extent to which you deployed each approach.

I would add that, just like change preference, we may have particular orientations, which represent a fairly consistent approach, in the absence of exceptional circumstances.

Having estimated the extent of the use of each approach, allocate each approach on Figure 6.2 a number between 1 and 20; mark that number on the appropriate line, and join the lines (as on Figure 6.1) to produce your profile.

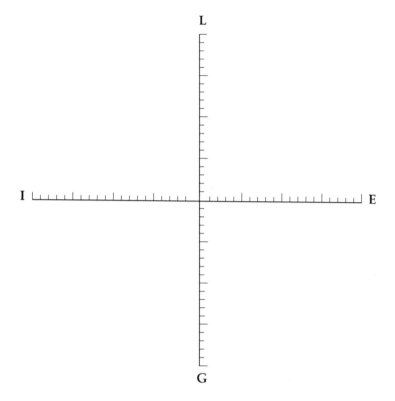

Figure 6.2 *Your profile.*

Your colleague's assessment

The appendix sets out the inventory that your colleague will complete. Before you do anything, we need to think through one or two important aspects.

You are persuading your colleague to make a change in the very act of asking him or her to complete the inventory. How are you going to tackle that?

- 'Fill this in and return it to me tomorrow.'

    This is an INCENTIVES approach! Implicitly we are saying 'I am your boss, and so you do as I say without asking questions'.

- 'I am looking at how I persuade other people to do things, and need you to fill in this form so I can compare what I think with what you think. Would you fill it in for me and return it tomorrow?'

    This is a LOGICAL approach.

■ 'Charles, do you think it is important that we have an effective business relationship? ... You do? I agree. Now I have come across what is called a Persuasion Inventory, which will enable us to see what sort of approaches I use when persuading you to do something. I have had a stab at working out how I think I go about it. Would you fill in the form, and return it to me so that I can find out how you see my approach? ... You will? Thanks. Then I'll share the results and we can have a chat about how we can make sure the relationship is more effective.'

This is an EMPATHY approach, and more time-consuming!

■ 'We all know that our mission is to serve the client first and not last. I've come across an Inventory which will help improve the effectiveness with which we serve the client. It looks at how I persuade you to do things. Could you fill it in and then, when I have looked through the results, we can have a chat about improving our approach as a team?'

This is a GROUP approach.

I leave it to you to determine your approach, though I would mention one golden rule for persuading another to make a change, to do something different. This is PBA, or Perceived Balance of Advantage.

An individual will always be persuaded to do something, to make a change, if, at any time during the discussion he or she PERCEIVES a net balance of advantage in the proposal being put forward.

As we have already discovered, managing perceptions and setting expectations are key to obtaining growth from change. How to improve our ability is part of the next chapter. However, recognition of their importance and the PBA rule is an excellent first step.

Before approaching the colleague you have selected, I would point out that:

■ The appendix in its entirety contains all the information that your colleague needs. It has been written from his or her perspective.

■ The inventory has been structured so that only you will understand the answers. You should be in control, when taking a step like this. All your colleague does is tick the A for agree box or D for disagree box, without knowing what the answers mean.

At this stage, you should select the lucky person, approach her or him, explain what you want done and why, hand over the Persuasion Inventory, agree what will happen after the completion (if you have decided on using an empathetic and/or group aspect) and await the return of the completed form. While it is worth continuing to read the book, the scoring, analysis and action planning clearly cannot take place until the completed form has been returned to you.

Scoring the answers

I have now made the assumption that you have the completed form at hand. Please examine the numbers set out below.

3 6 12 13 17 22 27 29 35 38 41 45 51 53 58 61 67 70 75 78 ☐ I

4 5 11 14 18 21 25 31 33 37 43 47 50 56 57 63 68 71 74 79 ☐ L

2 8 10 15 20 24 28 30 36 40 42 48 49 54 59 62 65 72 76 77 ☐ E

1 7 9 16 19 23 26 32 34 39 44 46 52 55 60 64 66 69 73 80 ☐ G

TOTAL = ___

Each number corresponds to the same number in the questionnaire. The numbers have been divided into four sets, as each set examines the key aspects of a persuasion approach: incentives, logic, empathy and group. All you need to do is to circle each number, whenever the statement corresponding to that number has been given a tick in the A or agree box (ignore ticks in the D or disagree boxes). When you have gone through the 80 answers, and circled all the A numbers, then add up the number of circles in each of the classifications I, L, E and G.

Check that the grand total corresponds to the total number of As given by your colleague, and then transfer the individual I, L, E and G scores to the appropriate section of your profile on Figure 6.2 and draw the link lines to complete the picture. I suggest you use a different coloured pen from your own assessment so that any differences are clear.

Interpretation

Only you are looking at the results, therefore only you will know whether there is a matching and no surprises, or a mismatch and what you perceive as good news or bad news. There tends to be the full spectrum of results from no surprises to good or bad news.

My most recent use of the inventory at the time of writing was with a programme of partners from a firm of city lawyers, who completed the full inventory on themselves as well as getting senior assistants to complete it on them.

For a few, there was a reasonably close matching (within three points) over all categories. One or two had a mismatch in one category. One was perceived as much less empathetic than he saw himself and one as much more, and so on. One was remarkable. The individual was a departmental head and I kept a record of his scores:

CASE STUDY

	I	*L*	*E*	*G*
Partner	13	14	13	12
Assistant	8	18	6	5
Difference	5	(4)	7	7

The partner saw himself as using all the approaches, and the assistant only one—logic, both factual, prejudicial and competitive. This sort of gulf is rare, but does happen. Nevertheless, discovery, however much bad news, is essential to growth.

To help interpretation, we make the connection between persuasion and leadership.

Persuasion and leadership

The way we persuade indicates how we lead. Figure 6.3 shows the four leadership approaches, which correspond to development levels. So we have 'command and control' for security, 'control and support' for self-esteem, 'questioning coach' for promoting growth with an individual emphasis and 'visionary team' for promoting growth with a team emphasis.

Assuming there is no big difference in perception, so that both you and your colleague agree as to the shape of the profile, there are still two questions:

1. 'Am I using an approach appropriate to the maturity or development level of this particular follower?'

2. 'Even if I am, should I try to change so that I increase the ability of the individual to gain growth?'

For instance, this might mean planning a gradual move from 'command and control' to 'questioning coach', as the follower's competence and confidence increases with your help. In persuasion terms, this is a move from a significant use of incentives and logic (which means that we stay with our agendas and try to persuade him or her to do what we want), to a greater use of empathy and group (so that our company's agenda becomes more prominent and we understand and respect the agenda of the follower).

There is another question, that would need a lot more work to answer, but may be perceived as being worth the investment of time:

3. Do I have a generic style with all followers (and peers and my boss for that matter) or do I have different styles for different people at different levels, and do I have the right approaches?

There are very positive characteristics of executives coming on our Senior

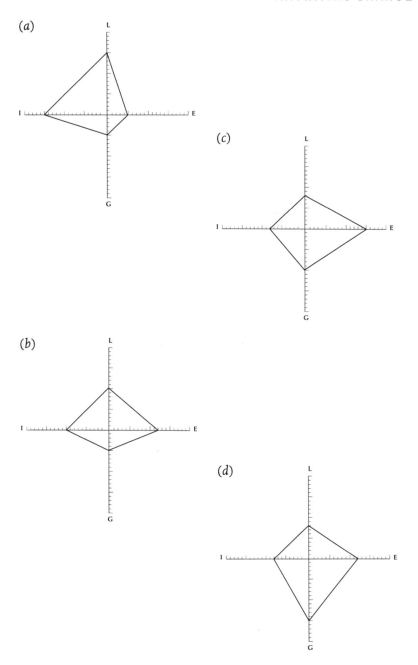

Figure 6.3 *Leadership approaches: (a) 'command and control'; (b) 'control and support'; (c) 'questioning coach'; (d) 'visionary team'.*

Executive programme. Generally, there is a strong desire to learn, and an openness to learning, coupled with a fine judgement and criticism of the quality of the resources provided. There is a willingness to recognize and develop weaknesses, and identification with the need to improve leadership competence on the back of increasing self-awareness, skill-development and confidence.

As the programme develops and barriers tumble, one major concern emerges: the relationship with the boss. It may be your concern as well. A powerful way of improving that relationship (and all relationships are capable of improvement) would be to ask your boss to fill in the form, where he or she is considering your persuasion and leadership approaches with your own followers. Your boss is likely to be easily persuaded to do this:

- Improving your relationship with subordinates helps the boss.

- Your own relationship with the boss is not being examined directly, though that could emerge if you were proactive in any subsequent discussion of your boss's conclusions.

- Your boss is not being asked for a self-appraisal but to judge you—and bosses tend to be happier doing that!

Levels of commitment to change

Before looking at the connection between persuasion and change preference and at initiating change for ourselves, it is worth considering the levels of commitment to change we generate according to how we persuade (see Table 6.2).

Table 6.2 Levels of commitment to change

Development level	Classification	Approach	Result	Duration
Security	'Stern parent'	I, L 'Control'	Do without commitment or understanding	Until escape
Security and self-esteem	'Strong leader'	G, I, L 'Inspire and control	Do with commitment but without understanding	Until retirement or removal of leader
Growth	'Questioning coach'	E, L, G 'Involve and explore'	Do with commitment and understanding	Permanent

Stern parent

The lowest level of commitment generated is what I have called 'stern parent'. This is where we are dominant in the I and L approaches to persuasion. We know the questions and we know the answers. It is up to our followers to do what we tell them to do. Because of the positional power we hold, we shall be 'obeyed'. There can, of course, be considerable subtlety in the way we use this approach, often not at the conscious level, as we have absorbed and automatically use the political and language skills that reflect the norms of behaviour appropriate to our organizational culture.

Indeed, many gurus such as Harrison and Peters see parent–child relationships at the heart of many western company cultures, a reality exacerbated by the recession and the need to fight for survival. It is a historic approach that is changing as the father-dominated family unit, from whence it comes, is disappearing.

It can be very effective, especially in the short run. However, as suggested previously, it may be less effective in the long run and has two fundamental drawbacks:

1. *It is not very efficient.* If the followers have a high need for security, they will respond but their heart won't be behind their actions, there will not be full commitment, and they won't fully understand what they are doing. If the followers are operating at higher development levels, then the response is often 'word only' and they proceed to do their own thing.

   The leader finds, much to his or her considerable annoyance, that the things that should be done are not done or are done badly. This creates a vicious circle of misconception, combined with a leader who is checking and chasing, forced to have too much of a hands-on implementation role, rather than a hands-off strategic role.

2. *It is not very effective.* With different roles and responsibilities appropriate to different jobs and different levels, the goals and targets need to be different. As we have discovered with the 'dilemma of change', a unidirectional approach is not appropriate. The 'stern parent' tries to force the troops, whether a small team or a whole company, to implement his or her answers. That will be ineffective.

Strong leader

I have called the next level of commitment 'strong leader'. This is where the I and L approaches are supplemented by some group aspects, particularly the creative and visioning skills.

The 'strong leader' is the current and historic model of good leadership.

A bad recession brings a whole nation down a development level. It is no accident that John Major has been heavily criticized for lack of vision and lack of strong leadership–taking decisive action and exercising control of cabinet and party alike.

We are all capable of being inspired for good or ill by a strong visionary leader. History, both national and corporate, is strewn with examples of strong visionary leaders who have inspired, controlled and moved mountains. Our self-esteem is developed by identifying with the leader, sharing his or her vision and values, and being part of the implementation of the vision.

It is very dangerous, as we all know. From the perspective of managing change, it cannot be successful in the long term, because the vision dies with the leader, and because it is unidirectional. The leader tries to define the future, which cannot be defined in a world of change.

The fundamental difference between the 'stern parent' and the 'strong leader' is that the latter can achieve what the former wants to achieve but cannot.

As regards the commitment of the follower, then that is given but full understanding cannot be. At the end of the day, we can follow our own dreams better than those of someone else, even if we have borrowed them for a while.

Questioning coach

The deepest level of commitment is that generated by the 'questioning coach'. His or her approaches are a mixture of logic, empathy and group, with very little incentives. It is not a purely individual approach, as there is a strong team dimension. The team as a means of achieving individual growth is examined in Chapter 8.

If our leader has provided us with an environment where we can explore and share, where we can create and support, where we can take risks without fear of ridicule, knowing there is a soft landing if we fall, then we can dream dreams that we can make a reality, and be relentless in pursuit of their achievement. We shall be committed to action and shall fully understand what to do, how to do it and why we are doing it.

However–and there is always a 'however'–this entire vision is predicated on both ourselves and our leader being capable of operating for sustained periods of time at growth level–and that may remain a dream.

As mentioned in the first chapter, a critical concern for leaders initiating change is the environment in which individuals operate. The more we can create an environment that is positive to change, the more growth will be obtained from change. We can easily underestimate the power we have in creating the right environment, simply because we do not proactively think of environment as a strategic tool at our disposal.

If we encourage explicitly certain types of behaviour, then they will take place.

A partner in a large firm of accountants was in charge of one of their local offices. She believed that one way to create a positive approach to change was through humour. So, she both 'preached and practised' humour, telling old staff and new staff alike that this was important and was to be encouraged. It worked. Not only is the atmosphere warm and friendly, but many staff have come up with many new ideas to improve customer service.

CASE STUDY

Persuasion and change preference

Is there any correlation between our change preferences and our persuasion approaches? Not necessarily. The focus of each is different: one is a preference and the other an actual approach, specific to a given individual. However, there may be a correlation where our change preferences are matched by our actual approaches to managing change. If that is the case, then the probability of correlation is high, because when we are in a leadership role, we are more likely to behave as we want to than in any other role. It would be worth comparing the two profiles.

So, if we have a high NC score, then we are likely to demonstrate a high degree of incentives to ensure that we can control others affected by change. If we have a high LD score, we are likely to have a high use of logic, when persuading others to change.

Equally, if we are People Focused (PF) when reacting to or initiating change, we are likely to adopt an empathetic persuasion approach to others. The correlation is least with PC, where if we are strong in that, we may not have a strong group persuasion approach, although we are likely to be high in the creativity/vision aspect.

Initiating change for ourselves

In this final section, we look at how we can most effectively initiate a major change for ourselves, building on the thoughts already expressed in this and earlier chapters. Rather than talk in pure theory, I shall be pragmatic and take as an example a specific change, where we have begun to think we might want to leave our current employers. Job mobility was on the increase in the 1980s, put on hold in the recession, and is likely to return with growth. I am talking about a voluntary exit in the sense that we have neither been made redundant nor perceived that as a likely event in the short to medium term.

Before we develop a process model, let us pull together some of the learning from earlier chapters, as well as bringing into play some new thoughts:

- Maximum AAAAAGH before the SO! We should carefully and deliberately formulate and implement our strategy. Time should be the least important concern: 'Decide in haste, repent at leisure.'

- The very fact that we are contemplating a move suggests that there is some negative emotional thinking towards our current job, whatever the reasons. These could be cultural, poor relationships with key players, recognition of becoming plateaued, lack of stimulation or too much stress and strain, or a combination. We know that we need to control our emotions and to force ourselves into a PC/LD mode, i.e. create and evaluate options.

  The grass is rarely greener on the other side, if it makes us sick on this side. Many departures are voluntary in a technical sense only. They have been the result of negative emotions. If we are, or can put ourselves, in a strong position in our current organization, then we'll make a much better choice when we change.

- A change of job also has a fundamental impact on our families. Such a change should not be contemplated without careful thought as to the alternative possible futures. This is a critical part of exploration. It is not alternative jobs we should look at initially but alternative futures. We need to go through a visioning process, taking ourselves away from the immediate present. A useful question is: 'What will be my vision and values in ten or fifteen years time?' It is a question we are often too busy to ask ourselves, but is one that is relevant even if we are happy with our lot, especially when the time horizon takes us into retirement!

CASE STUDY

Marion was a high-flier, already a senior manager in a large company at the age of 28. She was married to a successful man, and they enjoyed a very high standard of living—nice house, multiple exotic holidays and the like. As the result of attending a strategy programme, she asked herself the 10 to 15 year question as well as considering the corporate angle.

She was happy in her job, and did not want children, partly because she did not see herself as maternal, and partly because she didn't want to give up her career or find herself no longer in the top-tier (she was a realist!). Looking ahead, she would see herself reaching her career goals within the decade, and perhaps wanting to do something different. She recognized that there was a possibility she might want children, but saw the constraints as too great. She felt strongly that if she did have a child, she would want to care for it full-time in the early years. She also had a strong desire to increase her knowledge and learning, having missed out on a degree.

In this case, the solution was very easy. This was not to take any decision now, but to ensure that when decisions were required, they could be effectively made. She was lucky. The decision she took was to go into a high savings mode—cut the standard of living down significantly, but not ridiculously. There was the capacity for considerable saving and investment. If she decided in her late thirties to become a full-time mother, she could, as there would be the financial back-up plus a proven ability to live on one wage or one and a quarter for the previous ten years!

Alternatively, if there was no desire for children, she could give up her career and become a full-time mature student without any financial worries.

Her only issue when she returned home was to persuade her husband to make the change in lifestyle.

One of the lessons of this story, a point already made, is the need for support. Do not change jobs without seeking and obtaining the views of all those you can trust.

We have learned that part of effective change management is to be flexible and adaptable. We need to be what is termed 'strategically opportunistic'. In the context of a possible job move, that means testing the water. A well-known firm of executive recruitment consultants, GHN, gave a group of executives what many felt was sound advice:

Even if you are happy where you are, circumstances can change. Be prepared. As a deliberate policy, maybe once a year, test the marketplace. You will learn how to write a decent CV. You will learn how to have an effective interview. You will learn your market value. You may well find that, as you don't necessarily need or want the job, you will be offered it! You will develop competence and confidence, and you may get the perfect job, you didn't know you wanted.

In terms of process model, it is simply one of questions, answers and actions, which is iterative over time. There can be a tendency to explore and analyse too much, avoiding actually doing anything. One of the learning points from respondents to the questionnaire, when initiating change, was 'go for it'. Another, derived from the first chapter, was to break down the change into component parts, phased in gradually over time by a series of strategically necessary actions. This ensures flexibility, reduces the uncertainty factor, and increases the probability that the outcome of change will be less unpredictable and produce more personal growth.

The key questions and some specific answers, using the possible job move as an example, are:

Q1. *What are the specific reasons for contemplating the change?*
- Working too hard.
- Poor relationship with new boss.
- Could be plateaued.

Q2. *What stops us making the change?*
- Unsure of what job we want.
- Lack of support.
- Don't know our value in the marketplace.
- Lack of experience/confidence in the recruitment process.

Q3. *What needs to be done to progress matters?*
- Provide plenty of time both for planning and implementation.
- Talk to people, whom we trust.
- Increase the quality of the existing job.
- Develop a 10/15 year view of what we want to be doing and why.
- Test the marketplace.

Q4. *How are we going to proceed?*
- Set a time-limit for the change to have been completed or abandoned e.g. 2 years with reviews every 6 months.
- Determine who we shall talk to, and at what stage in the process.
- Formulate plans to reduce workload, and improve relationship with the boss. Later, say in six months, confirm promotion prospects. (A critical point. The order of actions is important. Feelings that one is plateaued can often be based on valid perceptions of the organizational view, particularly the boss's. It is counter-productive to deliberately confirm a negative reality and thereby precipitate an emotional response to initiating change. Wait until the action plan to change perceptions has been implemented before clarifying the position.)
- Begin to consider what kind of long-term future we would like for ourselves. We need to be objective and identify what have been the drivers in our career to date, and whether, taking a long-term perspective, they will not alter. We need to develop a vision that excites and the values that support it. We should involve our 'nearest and dearest'. (It is important to involve the family in the decision-making process, as they will be affected by any changes you make. There will also be people—close friend(s) or trusted working colleague(s)—who will provide a support service but are not affected by the outcome, and so can be fully objective. These are the people referred to in the second point above.)
- Start looking at job adverts, applying only for those that have considerable appeal. Research into what we need to do to tap into the non-advertised job market.

Q5. *In what order are we going to proceed?*
- Write out an overall strategic plan, prioritizing action areas and relevant actions, and recognizing the need for a phased and gradual approach. For instance, the immediate priorities should be

developing the plan and actions to reduce workload (creating more time to think and reducing stress) and improve the relationship with the boss. These may well be linked, and initial success will provide an enormous psychological boost. Paradoxically, this may not reduce the desire to leave. Once we contemplate change, and plan for change, a natural momentum towards change is created, which can be given a significant boost when the visioning process has started. From experience with a number of executives, once they look up, they tend to look for 'growth' level development, and recognize that they have been locked into value systems to promote self-esteem. They want to modify them to achieve growth for the future.

Changing the dimensions

Finally, by using a thoughtful, planned approach to initiating change, we are managing the dimensions of the relevant variables for growth:

1. Phasing in gradually.

2. Explicitly managing our own expectations and those of others.

3. Reducing the significance, by breaking the change down into its component parts.

4. Providing time so that the change will not be sudden.

5. Moving towards a higher development level to increase the probability of growth.

6. Promoting discovery, so that when the change occurs it will connect to the present and the past.

7. Managing perceptions for ourselves and others to ensure that the change is perceived positively.

Key point summary

■ When persuading others to change, combinations of different approaches can be adopted. Use can be made of: *incentives*–positively (the carrot) or negatively (the stick); *logic*–factual and rational or based on opinion or prejudice; *empathy*–displaying understanding and respect; or *group*–creating or using a common understanding of a shared vision.

■ The persuasion profile may be consistent over time with different people in different situations, or may vary. The greater the dominance of one or more persuasion approaches in a given profile, the more consistency there is likely to be.

■ We do not always see ourselves as others see us, which is why it is important to ask a subordinate to fill in the detailed inventory, so that any perception gaps can be identified and eliminated, enhancing the relationship as a result and enabling both parties to gain growth out of an actual change—a change in an important business relationship.

■ A useful rule in persuading someone to change is PBA or Perceived Balance of Advantage: *An individual will always be persuaded to do something, to make a change, if, at any time during the discussion, he or she PERCEIVES a net balance of advantage in the proposal being put forward.*

■ By looking within the answers from a subordinate, any specific orientations within each approach can be uncovered.

■ As the relationship with the 'boss' is important, the inventory can be used to enhance the relationship by asking the boss to complete the inventory on how we persuade our subordinates, and discussing the results.

■ Persuasion approach indicates leadership style: 'command and control' relies on significant use of incentives and logic; 'control and support' deploys incentives, logic and empathy; and 'questioning coach' uses logic, empathy and some group persuasion.

■ Persuasion and leadership approaches should be flexible and vary according to the development level and experience of the follower. With inexperienced or insecure followers, the initial approach should be 'command and control' moving through 'control and support' to 'questioning coach'. This enables followers to develop competence and confidence in themselves.

■ The effectiveness of persuasion will vary according to the persuasion approach. Operating as 'stern parent' with reliance on incentives and logic will produce superficial commitment to action and poor execution.

As a 'strong leader', adding the visionary aspect of group to incentives and logic will improve both commitment and implementation, but the individual just becomes an instrument to execute the persuader's will, without the full understanding that comes from belief generated from within. The 'questioning coach' with high empathy, rational logic and the creative aspects of group will enable the follower to explore and discover and will produce full commitment to action as well as understanding in execution.

- When persuading others to change, it is important to create a positive environment beforehand. Humour can be a powerful tool in generating such an environment.

- There can be a correlation between change preference and persuasion. When we are in our leadership role and feel comfortable, we are likely to initiate change according to our preference, deploying the persuasion approach that corresponds to the given change preference: incentives when in NC mode; logic when LD mode; empathy when in PF mode; and the creative aspects of group when in PC mode.

- When initiating change for ourselves, we should:
  —carefully formulate and implement the strategy;
  —provide plenty of time for this process;
  —identify and try to reduce or eliminate any negative emotions towards the status quo;
  —carefully explore all alternatives to the change contemplated to avoid 'deciding in haste and repenting at leisure';
  —try to generate a long-term vision so that any change can be put into a long-term context and we can ensure it is consistent with the long-term goals, which we may not hitherto have explicitly determined;
  —involve those we trust in our thoughts to gain a broader and balanced perspective on the change, and to ensure that we are supported through the change;
  —develop an action plan.

- The specific questions that should be asked and answered, when initiating change are:

  Q1. What are the specific reasons for contemplating the change?
  Q2. What stops us making the change?
  Q3. What needs to be done to progress matters?
  Q4. How are we going to proceed?
  Q5. In what order are we going to proceed?

- Looking at the variables and dimensions of change, the requirements to guarantee growth out of any change we contemplate making for ourselves are:
  —phasing in gradually;
  —explicitly managing our own expectations and those of others;
  —reducing the significance, by breaking the change down into its component parts;
  —providing time so that the change will not be sudden;
  —moving towards a higher development level to increase the probability of growth;

—promoting discovery, so that when the change occurs it will connect to the present and the past;

—managing perceptions for ourselves and others to ensure that the change is perceived positively.

Your own points

Developing skills

Introduction

This chapter focuses on key skills that will help us get growth out of change. One key requirement in an environment of change is to have a Positive Creative (PC) approach. We therefore look at how we can improve the flow of ideas from both an organizational and individual perspective. The more we are able to explore, challenge and change the nature and direction of change, the more growth will be achieved.

The other key skill areas covered are concerned with the people who are involved—ourselves and others. As initiators or agents of change, the greater our ability to manage expectations and improve perceptions, the better the experience and results of change. So we look at managing expectations, changing perceptions and promoting discovery.

The creative gap

Almost all companies, who express a view in their report and accounts or through their representatives, state that they are operating in a business environment of change, and must become more innovative and flexible as a key part of their strategic response to change.

This tends to be explicitly stated, as are connected themes like culture change towards continuous improvement or providing innovative solutions to changing customer needs. This can be seen as part of the response to the 'unpredictability' aspect of change.

What tends to be less explicitly stated is the need to increase the quantum of ideas that are generated and implemented by the organization as a necessary though not sufficient strategy towards achieving goals of innovation and effective culture change.

While targets are set in most areas where measurement is easy and where it is perceived necessary to motivate and reward staff, the number of ideas generated is not recorded, nor are targets set. I am not suggesting this crude approach is *the* answer but it is one of the many answers available to improve creative output.

It is worth noting that Edward de Bono, in a seminar I attended in 1989, pointed out that Toyota produced around 22 million ideas a year, which represented 326 per member of the workforce. He also mentioned that well over 90 per cent of these ideas were implemented.

While recording the numbers of ideas, setting targets, and introducing them into performance inducement systems may not be appropriate to many cultures, nevertheless the fact remains that the result of achieving the explicitly stated goals will be a continuous, significant stream of ideas that can be implemented.

Earlier chapters have shown that an approach to change that is gradual and strongly connected to the present works better than one that is sudden and disconnected. As mentioned in the first chapter, and exemplified by de Bono's figures, the Japanese have been particularly successful at this evolutionary rather than revolutionary strategic response to change.

Few companies can put their hands on their hearts and say: 'We are satisfied with the number and regularity of ideas that we generate to help us manage our changing and challenging business environments.'

There is thus a gap between desired and actual outcomes, when it comes to creativity. Let us look first at the reasons, before considering how the gap can be narrowed, if not eradicated.

Explaining the creative gap

There are a number of reasons why the gap exists, and I leave you to decide which hold true for your own company.

Now an idea implies doing something different from what is currently being done. So, if low motivation has been identified as an issue that is having an adverse effect on the 'bottom-line', then someone might suggest that a way to solve the problem (or improve the situation) is to pay staff more. This means doing something differently from the current situation. As an aside, we see that an idea is also a suggestion, a solution and an action. I shall return to this reality and the implication in the next section 'What is an idea?'.

Almost invariably in our cultures, an individual is held accountable for the status quo. If it is someone else's idea, the status quo individual might not see it as a helpful suggestion to solve a pressing problem, but as an implicit criticism of his or her performance. If the idea is seen in that way, and it is likely to be if the individual is operating at the security or self-esteem development level, it will die still-born if the originator is a 'subordinate'. The result is that employees, who come to their organization brimful of ideas in the morning, return home in the evening without ever having taken their hats off.

Eventually, they will not wear their hats to work.

Now, this is not always the case. There are cultures where ideas are encouraged, usually on an individual basis. There is a snag, however. The originator is asked to make it happen, to use his or her proactive nature and persuasive skills to go for it–develop and implement. The result is a sinking feeling in the pit of the stomach that having ideas means working harder. There has unfortunately been no accompanying comment to the effect that the individual's workload will be reduced to accommodate the development and implementation of the idea. The message the employee takes away is to avoid these nasty objects, called ideas, unless they reduce workload or enhance the employee's career.

Then there is the *creative* boss. If the status quo maintainer will not accept the ideas of others, he or she still needs to have ideas, as change is a reality to be managed. If that person is very creative, then he or she will have lots of ideas. However, as many managers and executives have expressed to me, it can be a bit of a disaster when the boss is the person with the ideas.

Unfortunately, having ideas is not the same as thinking strategically. The latter involves both generating a range of ideas for a given problem or issue, and thinking through the implications of each option, before deciding those options that are not mutually exclusive and can be implemented within the given time-frame using the resources that are available or can be made available.

In fact ideas people often give creativity a bad odour in the eyes of subordinates, harried from pillar to post trying to quash an idea they realize will not work or find some way out of different ideas to solve the same problem, generated at different times *and* mutually exclusive.

Then there is the *non-creative* boss. If the boss is not creative, then he or she will need to poach someone else's idea, usually the idea of a subordinate, as that is the safest policy. It may be a subconscious rather than conscious theft, but the result is the same. An idea, not fully comprehended, is implemented or passed up by the boss, who has not originated it, and the originator, the natural parent, is inevitably side-lined by the new parent who has adopted the child. This demotivates the subordinate employee and doesn't do much for the progress of the idea.

So, there are obviously many good reasons for the gap. This is unfortunate as there is a genuinely held desire by many decision takers to increase the flow of ideas to achieve desirable results at present–and perhaps necessary results in the future if competitors are first to close the creative gap.

In fact, this desire for more ideas is often expressed by the setting up of suggestion schemes and prizes for the best idea. Unfortunately, because the mind-set of protection of the status quo lingers on, what usually happens is that ideas, which represent genuine change, get lost, postponed, side-lined or rejected, and only those that achieve the politically acceptable cost-saving remain to be implemented.

Cost-saving on its own will not guarantee future growth, especially where the changing dynamics of the marketplace require changing attitudes and behaviours to improve the quality and effectiveness of interpersonal relationships and enable, among many benefits, a more flexible and creative approach to customers and product or service development and delivery.

What is an idea?

Unfortunately, the human desire to create difference and then treat difference as inferiority reduces creativity. Language assists this process: on the one side we have the minority—the creative types, talking about ideas, creativity, concepts and conceptualization, 'blue sky thinking' and brainstorming; on the other we have the majority—logical, pragmatic types, saying 'Stuff all this airy-fairy nonsense. Let's find practical solutions to real problems and get on with it.'

Now if the so-called creatives said 'Let us generate a range of alternative actions, and then select those that can be implemented within the constraints of time and resources. As a result we shall significantly improve the situation under consideration or reduce or eradicate the problem to be solved. What do you say?' The answer from the other 'camp' if unlikely to be 'stuff all this airy-fairy action thinking'.

And that is the reality. Ideas are simply actions. So, good-bye 'brainstorming' and hello to whatever you like—AAG (alternative action generation) or GAT (group action thinking) or simply IM (improvement meeting) or CIM (continuous improvement meeting).

One can understand how this language and divide has arisen. Ideas and suggestions, which convey a sense of incompleteness and lack of finality in terms of action are, within the limitations of a given culture, quite acceptable for employees to have. Deciding on action is the purview of the key decision takers in the organization, and not the rank and file. So 'I have an idea. Let us increase employee pay by 5 per cent' sounds less threatening than 'Let us take a different course of action (to the one we are currently taking). Let's increase employee pay by 5 per cent.'

Closing the gap

There is one sure-fire way which transcends almost all cultures—the setting up and effective deployment of small action thinking groups.

Before we look at that, I want you to use your imagination and visualize a specific scene. (Visualization is not only a powerful technique to improve memory but also to generate alternative actions.) This is a true story.

Structured action thinking

Imagine five executives in a wood, close to a hotel. They have just been presented with a problem, devised by my colleague David Butler. In front of them is a tree, which has a branch, to which is attached a pulley system. At the top is an empty petrol can with an exposed hole, and at the bottom is an identical can containing quite a few pebbles.

The task, to be completed in 20 minutes, is to reverse the position of the cans. There are constraints. A circle of around 25 feet diameter has been drawn round the tree, with the pulley system in the centre.

■ No one is allowed within the circle.

■ No direct contact is allowed with any object in the circle nor is any indirect contact, e.g. picking up a long stick and pushing the top can down.

So, after the briefing, this particular group started. One individual immediately suggested that they should fill the hole with stones. This was instantly accepted as the answer. The rest of the time was spent with two people searching for stones, of which there were hardly any, and the other three thinking up ways of getting one member close enough to the top to be able to drop the stones into the hole.

They failed.

It was a classic example of finding the 'one right answer' straight away—the one that was glaringly obvious, and then locking into comfortable activity to implement the solution.

Filling the hole with stones is what I call an *alternative action*. If you have identified an alternative action, there is an *action area*. In this case, it is obvious: filling the hole. However, if the problem was creativity in the company, and the alternative action suggested was 'introduce brainstorming', it is not so obvious what the action area is. That can be uncovered by asking: '*How would I classify* brainstorming?' It is a creative thinking technique.

Once you have identified the action area, you can then ask the question: '*What alternatives can I think of?*' In the case of the can problem, alternative ways of filling the hole are twigs, water, a stick and so on. '*What alternative techniques?*' leads to mind-mapping, structured action thinking (this process), force field analysis, Ishikawa fishbone analysis, visualization and so on.

But that is not the end. If you have identified an action area, you have not identified the *action concept* (sorry–an airy-fairy word has slipped in). This is uncovered by IGNORING THE ISSUE OR PROBLEM, and asking '*What is the purpose?*' The purpose behind filling in the hole is to *increase the weight* of the can. The purpose behind using creative thinking skills is to *develop expertise*. Once an action concept has been identified, you can then deploy the question: '*What are the different ways of ...?*' What are the different ways of enhancing expertise? We could develop techniques, we could hire experts, carry out training, use role models and so on.

Finally, there is usually more than one action concept. With the creativity problem, there is increasing motivation, increasing time spent, reducing resistance, establishing the need, improving the environment and so on.

So with a little structure, and a few appropriate open questions, individuals can significantly enhance their 'creative output'. This is quite a logical process, reinforcing the reality that the more logically developed we are, the more 'creative' we can be.

There is no divide. It's all in the mind!

The process is set out schematically in Figure 7.1.

Group action thinking

GAT is an incredibly powerful tool, which is easily introduced into most cultures.

However, as is always the case, to achieve optimum effect there needs to be structure, process and one golden rule. In the initial phase, which should have time limits when alternative actions are being generated, *no one is allowed to criticize by word or body language* the suggested action concept, action area or alternative action being put forward. (I shall refer to these three classifications to simplify matters as ideas!) There are three reasons behind this rule.

1. Criticism will stop the flow of ideas. In the extreme, criticism leads to the one right answer, that held by the most senior person present.

2. With a relaxed, humorous atmosphere generated, ideas which no one consciously had when entering the room will flow out. A creative fire can be lit, which criticism puts out.

3. As Edward de Bono has demonstrated, good ideas can be generated through deliberately reversing or exaggerating a key aspect of the issue under consideration. So 'silly' ideas must be tolerated and would be killed off under the withering fire of criticism.

ISSUE: IMPROVING THE FLOW OF IDEAS IN A COMPANY

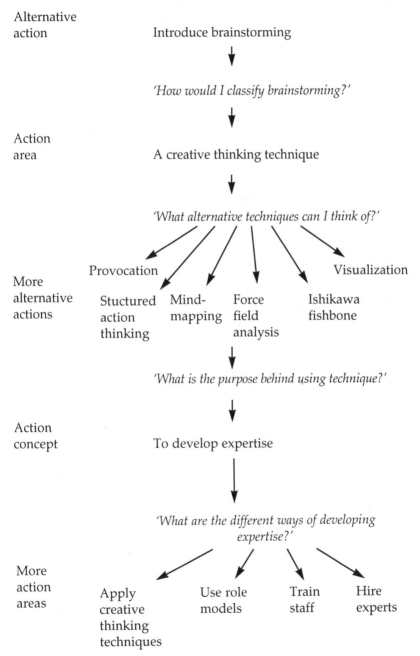

Figure 7.1 *Structured action thinking.*

EXAMPLE   Take an example from an actual GAT. During the generation phase, someone made the 'silly' suggestion that the chairman should be made a telephonist. Development of this suggestion by the executives involved led this company to introduce one week role-reversals between management levels. This was very effective in generating desired cultural change, enhanced relationships and more competent managers.

Not a bad return from one 'creative' action!

As regards structure and process, the individual introducing GAT needs to explain the rule and reason for it. A separate room (initially) is a good idea, as it helps remove status and is itself a change from the norm. Generating atmosphere with a few dry runs on some humorous issues is recommended. There can be an enormous difference in output between a group which is cold and hesitant and one that is relaxed and smiling.

A flip chart or whiteboard will be necessary so that there is a visual display of ideas *or* the group can stick post-it notes around the walls. In the former case there will need to be a scribe who is also a contributor. In the latter case the ideas should be verbally articulated as well as written down. In both cases someone needs to ensure that the 'no criticism' rule is followed.

Finally, there are some key benefits as well as things to avoid.

Benefits

■ The creative output will be far higher than that of any individual. We all have our mindsets, our limited background, experience and knowledge. By opening our minds, sharing our ideas and allowing those sparks to be generated, we all become more creative and the whole always exceeds the sum of the individual parts.

■ This also holds for development (identifying action concepts and action areas and hence more alternative actions) and evaluation. We can only tap into ourselves. The combined wealth of knowledge and experience of the group makes development and evaluation quicker and more effective.

■ Fundamental improvements in work processes will occur. GAT can be applied to issue identification, problem-solving, project definition, writing a scoping paper, planning and so on. It can be used for group tasks *and* individual tasks at any vital stage. Increasingly, it becomes informal and swift. Other team members are happy to be involved for four reasons:

1. It improves the efficiency and effectiveness of a colleague's output.

2. As it is reciprocated, it improves the efficiency and effectiveness of their own work.
3. The knowledge of the group about each individual's key work activities expands enormously. This makes it much easier to take up the reins, when a colleague is sick or on leave.
4. Team morale soars.

■ It is the way to generate a shared vision, common understanding, agreed objectives and a sense of unity and direction.

Things to avoid

There are quite a number of pitfalls to avoid.

NUMBER OF IDEAS
There can be a temptation to go for quantity rather than quality. One writer and practitioner proudly told his readers that he had achieved through one GAT over 100 restatements of the problem, and over 1000 ideas! Evaluation took months.

Quality is much more important. Often, you will get 20 or so alternative actions, half of which can be integrated into a structured action plan–great!

The 'no criticism' rule must take primacy, but it is worth creating an environment where there is no pressure for contribution and where silence is recognized as a creative act.

NUMBERS
Many experts recommend up to 20, acknowledging that some individuals will not contribute–presumably sacrificing atmosphere and the individual on the altar of quantity. GAT is best as a team or small group process, with numbers not exceeding 8 nor less than 4.

EVENT
GAT can be seen as a major and rare event, reserved for a major strategic issue, attended by a select group, usually off-site and expensive. There is a place for that, especially where the top team is involved. But it can give the wrong cultural messages–particularly that GAT is not a cheap, effective, work-based regular group activity.

ISOLATION
GAT is sometimes carried out in isolation. Evaluation is done later, occasionally by different people. GAT should be an integral part of problem-solving and action-planning, carried out by the same people, often in the same session.

In conclusion, managing change usually means taking risks. GAT is a risk-free change (if sold and introduced effectively) that will transform an organization.

Expectations

Setting and managing expectations is at the heart of relationship and change management. As often the case, lack of explicit recognition of their crucial strategic role denies their effective deployment as a formidable weapon in the individual armoury.

Let us take two similar examples.

EXAMPLE George is in the later stages of selling a high-value piece of business to a new client. It is Wednesday morning. 'So, when would you like the proposal by?' asks George. 'Well, as soon as possible. Could I have it by Friday?' replies the client. 'No problem. I'll get onto it straightaway, fax a copy to you on Friday, and post some extra copies as well, which you will get on Monday' states George eager to please this important 'prospect'. 'Fine. I look forward to reading it', the satisfied client replies.

George is a very busy man. This is not the only piece of time-consuming work he has promised. In addition to all his fixed appointments, he also has to draft an even more important proposal for his boss by the same deadline, already extended. He works Wednesday and Thursday evening, but has to phone up the client rather sheepishly late on Friday and explain that he won't be able to complete it until Monday. He achieves that, having to sacrifice a bit of the weekend, but it is a little bit rushed. There are quite a few typos and the costings don't add up.

George does not get the business.

EXAMPLE Karin is in the later stages of selling a high-value piece of business to an important new client. It is Wednesday morning. 'So when will you need the proposal?' asks Karin. 'Well, it will need to be discussed at the next board meeting. That is not until a fortnight on Friday. Papers are circulated the Monday before, and I'd like to glance through it first. Could you get it to me by Thursday week?' replies the client. 'Of course, no problem. How many copies would you like for circulation?' asks Karin. 'Ten' comes the reply.

Karin manages to complete the proposal, free of typos, by the same time as George did—the following Monday. She faxes one copy as a draft on the Monday, with a covering note that she will telephone on Wednesday to see if there are any changes her client might want. A productive telephone conversation leads to minor revisions on Thursday and 10 copies sent out, received by the client on the Friday and circulated to the board the following Monday.

Karin gets the business.

To help consider the implications behind these two stories, please refer to Table 7.1. There are some important general points to be made. The Japanese, according to our table, are into 'delight'.

Table 7.1 Managing expectations

Nature	Approach	Result
Explicit	Identifying, developing and exceeding needs	Delight
Explicit	Identifying and meeting wants	Satisfaction
Explicit	Failing to meet identified needs/wants: 'moving the goal-posts'	Dissatisfaction
Implicit	None	Event triggers gap, producing despondency

A Nomura Research Institute seminar was held in London in 1988. The British managers attending were quite taken aback by the arrogance of the Japanese hosts. This was particularly evident, when one speaker talked about their future strategy for the automobile. The speaker pointed out that the Japanese were seen by the West as imitators rather than innovators. Additionally, Western providers of luxury cars were confident that this was a segment that the Japanese would be unable to penetrate, as the West had years of experience and expertise the Japanese lacked.

CASE STUDY

The West was wrong on both counts. It was a matter of fact that of the 69 new chassis developed in the mass car market in the previous five years, 44 had been Japanese. More importantly, it took the West five years to produce a new chassis from scratch, whereas it took the Japanese only two and a half, thanks to their advanced process technology. As it would take the West 10 years to catch up, the Japanese could happily focus research efforts on the expanding luxury car market.

They had already started, and had spent billions of pounds on 'neural technology', which enabled replication of the human brain and the ability to focus on ergonomics, particularly identifying all the comfort factors, essential for luxury cars. Indeed, as an aside, they had produced a best-selling fan in their domestic market, which vibrated in accordance with one of Sibelius's pieces, which research had shown was very pleasing at the subliminal level.

Over the next years they would be successful in their planned expansion into the luxury car market, *as they would delight the customers, the West was trying to satisfy.*

Karin delighted where George failed to satisfy. Karin achieved this by exceeding the expectations she had set. The key was to identify needs and exceed those. It is much more difficult to exceed wants.

Needs change in the light of a proactive and creative approach by the 'salesperson' in the George and Karin example, or, more generally, by the initiator of change.

Another interesting point is the value of time. Time permits exploration and new ideas. It simply was not possible for George to do more than meet the wants expressed. He could only satisfy and never delight. Shortage of time so often leads to the 'one right answer' and to poorly implemented change.

This example was an actual client, but we have that laboured term 'internal clients'. We should consider those we involve in change as clients, and aim to identify and exceed their needs.

George was an example of where expectations were set explicitly and not met, as George moved the goal-posts. This leads to dissatisfaction. Moving goal-posts is one of the inherent problems that arises from the 'unpredictability' aspect of change. It is axiomatic that a changing environment leads to unanticipated change. The implication behind this is to set expectations that there will be a degree of uncertainty as to either timing or nature of outcomes.

Now, I am not talking about the short term (days or weeks) with clients or colleagues, as the nearer to the present the future comes, the more predictable that future is, but the longer term (months or years).

With the natural drive to remove uncertainty, we tend to set goals with too clear a definition too far away. We must deliberately build into the expectations we set, a degree of uncertainty to reflect the reality of unpredictability. Depending on the nature of the objective or event, this can be done by setting a range or a degree of probability.

So instead of agreeing a target with a subordinate of 175 sales to be achieved in one year's time, we agree that the target will be in the range 150 to 200. Instead of saying to a subordinate:

'If you meet the performance and development requirements of the job, you will be promoted in two years' time'

we say:

'If you meet the performance and development requirements of the job, the way things look at the moment, I anticipate you will be promoted any time between 18 months and 3 years. I cannot be any more precise, as you will appreciate. I cannot predict the future accurately, and changing events may change the time-scale. Conceivably, of course, promotions may dry up on the back of cut-backs and rationalization, which, for all we know, might be necessary somewhere down the line.

What we shall do is regularly review the situation. As time passes, we shall begin to see whether promotion is on the cards and when.'

As mentioned, unpredictability reduces the closer to the present the change comes. What we achieve by such an approach is to build into our expectations the necessary degree of uncertainty to reflect the reality of the unpredictability of future outcomes. At the same time, we provide a degree of comfort by building into the expectations the certainty of regular review.

Honesty is the best policy. More often than not, we do not know very much more than our staff!

The final approach in the chart is where expectations are simply not explicitly set. This can happen frequently in many situations. The result tends to be 'despondency' by the client or colleague, triggered by a specific event, which brings to the surface the gap that exists but has, until the event, lurked latent and unrecognized.

For example, in relationships with subordinates in some cultures, there is an absence of criticism or praise from the manager most of the time. Subordinates make assumptions that are not checked. They set themselves implicit expectations of their performance, as viewed by the highly significant individual in their career development—their boss.

At appraisal time there can be a rude awakening. 'You have failed to do this, and I am marking your grade down accordingly' or 'Your approach to clients is too abrasive. I am marking your grade down accordingly', says the boss. '*I did not realize*' or '*I assumed*' or '*I don't agree*' or '*I did not know*' or '*You should have told me months ago*' comes the reply. But, by that time, the damage is done—the subordinate's motivation is reduced and, perhaps, too much time has gone by for the manager to alter his or her mind.

And who is to blame—the poor leader or the passive follower?

- Many progressive companies have instituted quarterly, informal, but structured performance reviews to eradicate the problem of implicit expectations in the area of performance.

- Implicit expectations produce gaps in perception that reduce the ability to get growth out of change.

- Setting expectations explicitly, with regular review and feedback ensures there are no gaps.

Perceptions

Perception gaps occur because of a lack of communication. This increases the negative impact of change, because the event, like criticism or poor performance, is sudden *and* unexpected. Perception gaps also occur as a result of communication. We shall look briefly at how this happens and what steps we can take to reduce the gaps. The result is to improve communication and, hence, our ability to gain growth out of change. The model is shown in Figure 7.2.

You will notice that there are two gaps—the gap between conscious intention and manifestation (gap 1) and the gap between manifestation and the impact on the other party (gap 2).

As an example, let us take a situation where we want to persuade Sally, a colleague, to change the way she is managing a project.

Our conscious motivation or intention is to transfer a little of our expertise to Sally so that she does the project better. We shall assume that *we* are her boss, and are accountable for the results of the project—so there is an element of self-interest. We shall also assume that she is the project leader and we hold only a watching brief. She has been given both the authority and responsibility to manage the project team.

No gaps arise in the right environment with the right approach. Let us say that the words we use, with consistent non-verbal signals or 'body language', are: *'I have a good idea on how we can reduce the time taken to install the new network.'*

If this suggestion comes as part of a regular weekly review of the project with Sally, if there is an agenda where key aspects of the project are discussed, and if information technology (IT) is the item being discussed, then provided that our idea is sound it is likely to be gratefully accepted. There are no gaps. The suggestion is part and parcel of explicit expectations set, and is phrased in a positive non-critical way. Because the manifestation expresses the intent effectively, there is no gap 1. With the environment also right, there is no gap 2. We achieve our objective, which is to get Sally to 'change'—to do something differently from what she would have done without our effective intervention.

In the wrong environment, although there is no gap 1, we may cause a gap 2. We shall return to this when we look at gap 2. We now focus on the causes of gap 1.

Gap 1

Stress

We may be under stress, feeling irritable, in a rush and so on. So we say: *'The installation time for the new network can be reduced by 50 per cent. This is what you have to do ...'.* Interestingly, when under stress or in a rush, when we are feeling the pressure, there is a natural inclination to move to a more 'tell' style or 'command and control' leadership approach. As we have seen, the problem is that some staff will only verbally agree and ignore us afterwards, and others will do their level best to implement our

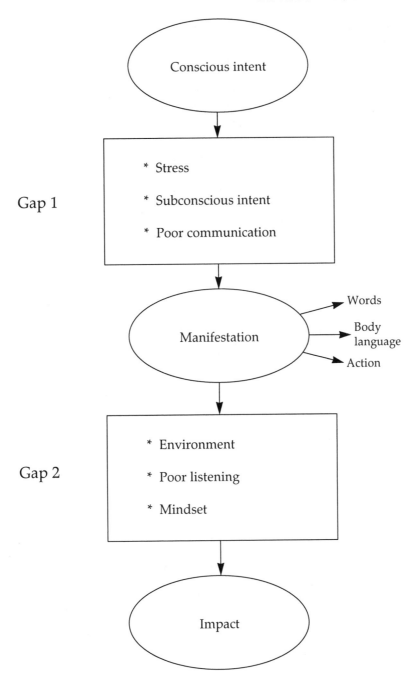

Figure 7.2 *Perception gaps.*

suggestions or 'instructions', but won't fully understand or 'own' the solution and so will implement them imperfectly.

In fact, we may well not bother with a face-to-face meeting and send a written communication to Sally, advising her of what to do to improve the management of *her* project. Putting yourself in Sally's shoes, would you see that intervention as a helpful suggestion, which acknowledges and respects her authority and competence as project leader? Yet that was the intent!

Incidentally, there are many executives who use written instruction as a matter of course, with no intention to upset or demotivate. They are unaware of the impact, because the follower is not prepared to volunteer feedback that is never requested. In any case, if feedback is ever 'requested', it will never be honest. If the employee is on the way out, honest feedback may be volunteered and ignored!

Subconscious intention

In Chapter 5 we saw that conscious intention may hide a subconscious or implicit intention that is more negative. So our conscious desire may be to improve the position, but to build self-esteem we also want to criticize. The way we behave manifests such hidden intentions. 'Sally, your plan to install the new network is flawed. I have come up with a way to reduce installation time by 50 per cent. This is what you have to do.'

Human nature being what it is, Sally is likely to pick the word 'flawed' as the key word in the sentences, and react negatively to what she perceives is implied criticism.

Poor communication

The third gap is simply poor communication. If we are the experts, and know more than Sally on IT matters (perhaps one of her team is the IT expert), then we may use language, jargon or concepts that she does not fully understand. She may perceive us as blinding her with science, or proving our superiority in the chosen area—none of which was intended. Unless she acknowledges her lack of understanding and seeks and receives clarification (and often people are reluctant to expose ignorance), then implementation of the change will be not fully effective, or the wrong change will be implemented—neither of which is a desirable outcome. To close any gaps:

■ We must recognize and try to eliminate stress, at least temporarily. Avoid the hasty memo or sudden intervention by telephone or 'dropping in'. In fact, it will significantly help our stress and that of the other party if we have a policy of proactively managing the environment so that it is conducive to the acceptance of change before we make our intentions known. (See gap 2.)

- We must deliberately use the 'assertive pause' not this time in reaction but before initiation—consciously consider our intention and motivations and try to identify and eliminate any critical aspects *before* we speak.

- We must try to avoid jargon and, as a matter of policy, check that the other party has understood what has been agreed to!

Gap 2

Now the impact can be different from the intent in three ways:

- Gap 1 (stress, subconscious intention or poor communication)—the gap between what we consciously intended and the actual manifestation of intent—produces an impact, necessarily different. Sally accurately responds to the behaviour manifested, as that is the explicit demonstration of intent. She will assume, because of the gap, an intent that is consistent with the manifestation, but not our actual intent. Hence the misperception that can be so damaging to relationships and to the effective initiation of change. In this case there is no gap 2.

- No gap 1, but gap 2. Manifestation of intent matches intent. However, the environment in which the interchange occurs, or the poor listening skills of Sally or her mindset towards the transmitter (gap 2) means that the actual impact is different from intent/manifestation.

- Then there is the cumulator. There is both a gap 1 and a gap 2. They can combine in an explosive way to lead to the most unfavourable outcomes, from a shouting match to employee dismissal.

We shall consider the cumulator later.

Environment

As already mentioned, the environment in which an interchange takes place is critical to the outcome. So if the message is delivered in a way that is consistent as to intention and manifestation, then the impact can still be negative because the environment is wrong.

Both us as initiators and Sally, the receiver, have a responsibility to pro-actively manage the environment. As suggested, we should avoid the unexpected such as dropping by or telephoning with a new idea. Sally also needs to be assertive when we enter the wrong environment and advise us that she is rushed off her feet, busy in a meeting, going to a meeting and so on.

Poor listening skills

Sally, at the receiving end, may not pick up the message correctly. There can be cause and effect with the environment—Sally is distracted by pressure of other work *or* fails to listen actively, only focusing on part of the message or picking up the wrong end of the stick.

This is no problem for us as initiators, provided we do not make assumptions that agreement means understanding, and ensure that those assumptions are checked. Although, in theory, we can be considered as not being responsible for the causes of gap 2, we need to be proactive to avoid the harmful effects that may result. It is the price paid for being the initiators, if success is desired, or simply the responsibility of good leaders, initiating change.

Mindset

People will often not believe the evidence of their own eyes. It happens in personal and business relationships. People come to expect what happened in the past, and pass judgements that become unwritten rules of behaviour towards the other person in the relationship. They do not notice change in attitude or approach. So, if they perceive an initiator of change as someone who has in the past criticized when suggesting change or told them what to do out of stress or communicated poorly, i.e. there has always been a gap 1, they may well react to effective communication of intent as if there were still a gap!

This is very difficult for us, as initiators, to respond to effectively: each of us is likely to think: 'Here am I trying to respect Sally's position as project leader, and suggesting a useful change in a positive way, and all she does is throw it back in my face. Well, I am not standing for that. Now, Sally, let me tell you …'

We receive an unexpected reaction, perceived negatively and move automatically into control mode.

[You may discover a direct way of handling this situation. All I can suggest is an avoidance strategy. If you, as initiator, ensure that the environment is right, that itself will begin to change the perceptions of the person with the negative mindset. Another approach would be to introduce GAT, so that one-to-one issues transfer to small group issues, and are solved effectively by the power of the GAT process.]

The cumulator

Our conscious intention is to make a helpful suggestion, but we criticize, and the intervention occurs in the wrong environment—in front of Sally's own subordinates. This is not deliberate—we have rushed in with a brainwave. The combination of gaps can produce explosive and damaging outcomes.

Such problems will be eliminated if we recognize that they can arise and have ensured that the right environment has been created before any exchange.

Promoting discovery

This is simply the most effective approach to managing change. It represents 'growth level' leadership, i.e. 'questioning coach' or QC. If QC wants to persuade an individual, or for that matter a small group, to make a change, then QC will succeed in those cases where the individual or individuals are not locked in security or low levels of self-esteem.

As already mentioned, the environment in which the interchange takes place will be important, as well as the expectations of the individual(s). It is the responsibility of QC to ensure that both variables have been managed effectively before the exchange takes place.

QC needs to have developed good questioning skills, be able to listen effectively, and have an open mind. On some occasions, the parameters of the change will be explored and stretched to such a degree that the actual change will be different from and better than the one QC initially contemplated. In other words, in promoting discovery, QC must recognize that he or she may also discover.

The approach will also reduce the negative impact of change involving a subordinate, which the organization has directed QC to 'impose'.

The reason the approach is so powerful and effective is that it enables individuals being persuaded to discover the changes for themselves in a way that is accepted. As mentioned in the Preface, QC believes in the acorn view of the individual and acts as the catalyst for discovery.

There is a gradual alteration in perception so that the 'persuadee' alters his or her mental model of reality, and moves from complete ignorance of the change (which if suddenly announced as a *fait accompli* and perceived negatively would mean passage down the reaction curve) to acceptance, and usually commitment, because of understanding of the need for change.

We shall look at two examples. You may recall the exercise, described in Chapter 4, with the land-skis where QC enabled discovery of a new principle eliminating the need for the groups to shuffle across the marker, improving their times as a result. The first example represents the approach a QC would adopt to enable effective discovery of the change.

We shall assume that the groups have carried out a fair amount of practice using the existing approach, which is to move the skis as fast as possible just past the marker, with well coordinated group 'walking', shuffle across, then turn collectively to face in the opposite direction back down the track and proceed as fast as possible to the finish line.

We also assume that after the latest run, where times have improved a little further, QC has called the group members (GM) together for a discussion.

QC: Well done, everyone. Each group has managed a new personal best. Your group from 58 to 55 seconds, yours from 53 to 49 and yours from 38 to 35. Let's have a discussion to see how you can all produce even faster times. Any thoughts?

GM: Well, practice makes perfect, they say. So if we practise more, we shall all get faster.

QC: True, very true. Let me ask you something. Can anyone remember the approximate times you managed first time round?

GM: Yes. All groups were over 2 minutes, and ours unfortunately over 3.

QC: Right. And how many runs have we had?

GM: Well, it is six I think. Yes, that's right, it's six.

QC: Before the last run, you were all under a minute. So in four runs you all improved over a minute. What about the improvement just now?

GM: Er ... 3 to 5 seconds.

QC: So what's the implication if we carry on practising?

GM: Marginal improvement.

QC: Exactly. Practise improves, but eventually the law of diminishing returns sets in—lots of practice for little absolute improvement. So how could you get a significant improvement?

GM: Try a different approach, I suppose.

QC: Yes. Any thoughts?

[*Pause.*]

GM: No, not really.

QC: OK. Let's try a different angle. Do you go at an even pace throughout?

GM: No. We start up, get into our stride, slow down for the turn and stop, execute the turn, start up again, get into our stride, slow down and then stop.

QC: And you much time is spent in the different phases?

GM: I don't know—but I could walk it at the approximate pace and time it.

QC: Fine. Go ahead.

[*Pause.*]

GM: Absolutely amazing. The turn takes up as much time as going to the marker and back. So, if we could speed up the turn somehow, we could see a big improvement.

QC: Quite right. The chain is as strong as the weakest link. It is always useful to find out exactly where the weak link is and strengthen that, and not just strengthen the chain as a whole. Any thoughts on that, then?

GM: Well, if the turn is causing all the problem, I wonder whether we need to turn. That sounds a bit silly. What am I trying to say? … I mean don't slow down, and go round in an arc, rather than stopping and shuffling across, everyone turning round and starting up again. It will probably take even more time, I suspect.

QC: No, you have hit the nail bang on the head. The best turn is, in a sense, no turn at all–just keep going round in an arc and back and you'll reduce time by up to 20 more seconds. Incidentally, I know you have all covered creative thinking, and how it is helpful to provoke the brain by reversal or illogical thinking. This is a classic case, where you all assumed you need to turn because of past experience. You find by unearthing the facts that the turn is pivotal, and the 'no turn' reversal concept leads to significant improvement. Let's try it out. OK.

GM: Yea. Great.

QCs have to be very patient, especially as often they do know the answer. The direct approach of: 'The way to improve is not to turn round at all but keep going in an arc. Off you go and try it out' is less successful, although less time-consuming.

Until the evidence is uncovered, no one appreciates how time-consuming the turn has become. Many will not believe. Some will accept because they trust the leader. For all, there will be a degree of reluctance to move from the known, comfortable and 'successful' approach to the untried.

Also, a mix of disbelievers and those taking it on trust are not, as a team, going to put the energy, effort and commitment to prove the leader right– see the next chapter on 'Growing the team'.

The self-discovery approach provides both understanding and commitment.

Come to think of it, you may recall that only one group actually followed the new principle. Even then, they lost time initially, in adjusting to a new pattern and finding the right arc and pace to proceed around it. What I had forgotten, until reflection produced re-discovery, was that the individual who came up with the answer was from that group, and that group had already bonded strongly and was performing the best. All groups had been subject to a series of changes, taken on trust as part of that day's programme. As we said in Chapter 1, if individuals or a group are subject to a series of changes with which they have not been involved, a resistance to change builds up. This is what happened for two of the teams.

The third was the exception because it was a performing team, and because one of them–and so all of them–discovered the new principle, believed in it and were prepared to have a go.

The second example is more practical, although the principles in the first example can be successfully applied to managing change in the workplace.

Here we take a situation where the chief executive officer has told a senior manager that one of his staff, who currently focuses on delivering the service with a little bit of selling, should have the emphasis completely reversed, as he is good at selling.

The CEO has a 'command and control' leadership style, and the senior manager cannot demur, although she knows that her subordinate neither likes selling nor sees himself as any good, and loves service delivery.

A typical approach (if somewhat exaggerated), where the senior manager replicates her boss's approach, after the subordinate is summoned to the office, would be 'Great news, Carole. The CEO is delighted with that sale you clinched last week, and so you are to move into sales more or less full time. Congratulations and good luck!'

We know the guaranteed reaction of Carole to a sudden, significant change, perceived negatively. If she stays with the company, she is unlikely to make a great salesperson for a very long time, if at all.

Let us assume that Carole's boss is, despite her own boss's style, a QC. As a QC, she will have created the right environment and managed expectations. So, Carole is having a fairly informal chat, which she expected, about performance and career options.

QC: So, Carole, let's consider how your role should best develop in the next year or so. As a starting point, let us consider what you do well. What are your views?

Carole: Well, er, delivering the service to the client. The exact nature of the service and timing of delivery is agreed in the proposal I get. I know our services backwards, my communication skills are good and I satisfy the client according to the agreed contract. What's more, I enjoy it, and the clients know I do, and that makes the service I provide even better.

QC: Agreed. There is no doubt that you perform very well in meeting the client's service needs. But what about selling? You do that well too.

Carole: Well I don't do much selling. And what I do is not proper selling.

QC: What do you mean precisely?

Carole: Well the business I get is nearly all from existing clients, where I have already proved my competence, and who appreciate our company. So it is easy to sell more of the same service or sell different services that my colleagues actually deliver. I tend not to follow up the leads that come in via the telephone sales teams. I'm not an aggressive, pushy type.

QC: No you certainly aren't. Let me ask you. Why do our customers buy our services?

Carole: Because they believe that our service will meet their needs, and will provide value for money spent.

QC: And who creates that belief?

Carole: Well, the salesperson, of course.

QC: And how does the salesperson create that belief, without which there won't be a purchase decision?

Carole: She builds a relationship and creates trust in herself as well as the service.

QC: Yes, good salespeople sell themselves. Most service decisions or employment decisions for that matter are made as a direct result of the quality of the relationship the salesperson or the prospective employee creates with the purchaser. People buy people not products. You have excellent skills in communication and developing relationships. So, Carole, are you good at selling?

Carole: Well, put like that, the answer must be yes. I hadn't really thought about it before in those terms. But, yes, you are right I am good at selling, but I prefer delivering the service.

QC: Naturally so, as you are good at that, comfortable with it and spend most of your time working in that area. But there is something else to consider. In your opinion, how many competent service deliverers do we have?

Carole: Well, I think the whole team is competent, which is one reason why we are getting so much repeat business.

QC: I agree. What about good salespeople, taking the definition we have agreed?

Carole: Well, quite a few aren't up to scratch. Organizationally, we are better at delivery than selling.

QC: Again, I agree. So, from an organizational perspective, which is the priority—finding a good salesperson or a good deliverer?

Carole: Well, obviously, a good salesperson. Just a minute, I begin to see where all this is leading. You want me to do more selling, don't you?

QC: Got it in one, Carole—and not just me, but our beloved CEO as well.

We shall leave the conversation there but the discovery that she is good at selling and that the organization needs her to sell, coupled with extra training on following leads and ensuring a gradual phased transition, should ensure that Carole, with some discomfort initially, will make the transition effectively and without reduction in motivation.

The QC approach is very, very powerful indeed. Yet there are few QCs in organizations. Cultural norms usually make the development of QCs difficult. Not that QCs do not flourish in any culture. It is just that they are not encouraged.

Key point summary

Creativity

■ For many organizations, there is a gap between explicitly stated corporate goals, requiring a steady flow of ideas that are implemented and the actual creative output of the organization or the number of ideas effectively implemented.

■ There can be a number of different reasons for a creativity gap:
  –Those responsible for the status quo may not encourage ideas, which necessarily imply a change to the status quo, as they are taken as criticizing the individual responsible.
  –Even with creative decision takers, there can be a lack of ownership by those required to implement them, as well as incompatible solutions to the same problem.
  –Where ideas are encouraged, it is usually on an individual basis, and individuals are reluctant to put forward ideas, because they are responsible for their implementation without reduction to their existing workload.
  –Conversely, decision takers can 'borrow' ideas from others, shutting out the originator and not fully understanding the idea. This can make implementation ineffective and the idea is abandoned as a result.
  –There can be an artificial divide and tension between the minority perceived as creative and woolly thinkers and the majority perceived as logical and action-oriented with rejection by the logical of ideas seen as 'airy-fairy nonsense'.

■ Ways of closing the gap are:
  –Recognition that ideas are action-oriented. 'Ideas' can be classified into action concepts, action areas and alternative actions.
  –Introducing group action thinking (GAT).
  –Encouraging logically based techniques like structured action thinking to progressively remove the artificial divide between so-called creative and logical thinkers.

Expectations

■ Expectation management of clients, whether internal or external, is the key to achieving growth from change.

■ In the short term, explicit expectations should be agreed and met, based on the recognition and development of need. This produces 'delight'.

- If expectations are explicitly based on wants, then only 'satisfaction' can be produced.

- In the long term, goals and objectives should not be too clearly defined, as the inevitable moving of the 'goal-posts' resulting from the unpredictability aspect of change causes 'dissatisfaction'—explicit expectations have not been met. Unpredictability should be explicitly managed by introducing up-front a degree of uncertainty as to outcomes, either as regards the event itself or by means of a target or time range. Uncertainty can be reduced over time by regular reviews.

- Not agreeing expectations explicitly should be avoided, as implicit expectations build a gap in perception. The existence and nature of the gap is triggered by a specific event. As the gap is usually perceived negatively, is usually significant, and the exposure by the event is sudden, passage down the reaction curve is inevitable, leading to 'despondency'.

Perception

- Gaps in perception can arise due to lack of communication and the development of false expectations. As mentioned, such gaps can be avoided by agreeing expectations explicitly and having regular reviews.

- Gaps in perception can also arise because of communication.

- There can be a gap between the conscious intention and actual manifestation of behaviour due to stress, subconscious intention or the poor communication skills of the individual initiating change.

- There can also be a gap between the manifestation of behaviour and the impact it has on the 'persuadee' due to the negative environment in which the interchange takes place, the poor listening skills of the other party or that person's negative mindset towards the initiator.

- Ways of closing the gaps are to ensure that the initiator has created the right environment and the right expectations before manifesting intention, consciously thinking about the likely impact in advance and structuring manifestation to match intent, as well as always confirming that the message has been fully understood and accepted.

Promoting discovery

- This is the most powerful way of getting growth out of change, because it enables individuals, who the initiator perceives need to change, to discover that for themselves. The individuals progressively change perceptions so that a change, which might be rejected or might demotivate because it is perceived negatively and/or is introduced suddenly, becomes perceived as necessary and its nature is understood, increasing significantly the probability not only of acceptance, but commitment through understanding.

■ The leadership approach is called QC or 'questioning coach'. The QC needs to have managed the right environment and expectations before initiating the voyage of discovery. The QC, operating at growth level of development, also needs good listening and questioning skills. An open mind is also essential, as the voyage of discovery can often be mutual, and the actual change discovered and agreed may be different from the QC's original expectations.

Your own points

Your action plan

You may want to focus specifically on improving the business relationship with the individual who completed the Persuasion Inventory for you.

Growing the team

Introduction

In this chapter, we move away from one-to-one interactions in change situations to group interactions. The focus is on how you, in your team leadership role, can produce an effective team. More specifically, we look at:

- The benefits of team-working

- The value of an effective team

- Problems with teams

- Team development

- Leading team growth

- Impact of change and reality.

Not all of us have enjoyed the experience of working in an effective team. The reason is simple. An effective team is a growth-level unit where all the individuals in the team are operating at the growth level. That is both rare to achieve and to sustain, but it is not impossible. More importantly, teams can operate at sufficiently high levels of development frequently enough to produce positive value, which justifies their existence. Equally, teams can operate permanently at a low level of development insufficient to justify their continuation—a waste of individual time, which goes unrecognized.

All of us carry inside our heads a model of effective team-working. This is because we have all, perhaps on a regular basis, experienced poor team-working. By looking at what does not work for us, we can develop a view of what does work and how it can be achieved—a process similar to developing a model for effective leadership.

So, at this stage, could you please reflect on your actual experience of working in groups and jot down a few thoughts in answer to the question:

What has annoyed you or caused problems for you, when working in a group?

We shall look at some answers in the section 'Problems with teams'.

The benefits of team-working

There are many research findings from many countries on the benefits of team-working. Quoting Anthony Montebello and Victor Buzzotta:

Companies that are willing to rethink old ways and develop teams can profit by increasing quality and productivity. And they can develop a workforce that is motivated and committed.

An American Society of Training and Development HRD (Human Resource Development) Executives received responses from 230 HRD executives about team-work results. The survey found that, of the respondents' companies:

- productivity improved in 77 per cent

- quality improvements were reported in 72 per cent

- waste was reduced in 55 per cent

- job satisfaction improved in 65 per cent

- customer satisfaction improved in 55 per cent.

Additional benefits cited were more efficient production scheduling, improved production goal-setting and increased ability of team members to resolve their own disputes.

Quoting Tom Peters, from his book *Thriving on Chaos: Handbook for a Management Revolution*:

I observe the power of the team is so great that it is often wise to violate common sense and force a team structure on almost anything ... companies that do will achieve a greater focus, stronger task orientation, more innovation and enhanced individual commitment.

It is a characteristic of companies in recent years as they respond to the 'unpredictability' aspect of change to significantly increase the number of teams in operation: board teams, project teams, ad hoc teams, functional and cross-functional teams, departmental teams and so on.

Creating a structure does not, of itself, produce effective teams.

The corporate division of a large financial services group reorganized as the result of the findings of a prestigious consultancy firm they had hired to produce a report on the best way forward. Previously, they had been structured in product groupings with product team leaders, managing very hierarchical 'teams'. This had produced poor customer service, with customers particularly annoyed by being approached by different teams at different times, selling their particular products.

Within a few months they had reorganized into customer groups containing a number of specialists over the range of products. There was a significant flattening of the hierarchy with the removal or coalescing of grades. An individual team member of the previous product group could find herself promoted to customer group leader, with no leadership experience. Equally a specialist product leader, used to a 'command and control' leadership approach, found himself called upon to adopt a more flexible leadership style to respond to being in charge of experts outside his own knowledge base, as well as the need to form informal networks across the new customer groupings, where he had no leadership authority.

No training or support was provided. The anticipated benefits of improved quality of service, enhanced customer satisfaction and increased business flows did not materialize as the result of this major structural change.

Indeed if we look at the reverse side of the research findings quoted:

- 23 per cent of companies saw no increase in productivity

- 28 per cent did not enjoy quality improvements

- 45 per cent did not reduce waste

- there was no improvement in job satisfaction for 35 per cent

- 45 per cent saw no increase in customer satisfaction.

The lessons, therefore, from this and similar surveys are two-fold:

1. Team-working is the way forward for companies to get growth out of change.

2. Companies that implement a policy of training team leaders to produce effective teams will generate the benefits to be derived from team-working.

The value of an effective team

From the organizational perspective, the core value of an effective team is that it produces better results more quickly than could the individuals operating on their own. It is both a more efficient and effective unit.

The superior quality and quantity of output is referred to as 'synergy'—

the combined effect that exceeds the sum of the individual effects. Put simply, if there are a group of five individuals, operating as an effective team, then the laws of mathematics are broken as 1+1+1+1+1=7!

We have seen that GAT (group action thinking), if properly and effectively introduced, produces creative synergy–more and better ideas than the sum of the ideas of the individuals thinking on their own.

Effective teams will deploy GAT as an integral part of the problem-solving process (see the section on 'Leading team growth').

At this stage, I would like you to consider your answer to one other question.

Imagine that you have crash-landed in the subarctic. Fifteen items have been rescued before the plane sank. In the actual exercise, initially working on your own, you would have to decide your priorities: which is the most important item for your survival, which is the second most important, and so on. Then as a group member, you would have to agree to a single new list of priorities, before comparing with the expert rankings and seeing if there has been an overall improvement–measuring the degree of synergy, if any. The question is:

'What does the group need to do, how can it achieve it and what behaviour/ approaches should individuals adopt to guarantee the creation of synergy?'

We shall look at some answers in the section 'Leading team growth'.

From the individual perspective, the team is a means of achieving individual growth faster and more effectively than if an individual developed in isolation or relied purely on one-to-one interactions.

However, for those of us, and there will be many, who have never experienced effective team-working, that statement can only be taken on trust or, more likely, treated with a high degree of scepticism or downright disbelief.

This is a critical individual and organizational issue.

Many key decision takers in companies have reached the top through a focus on the individual (themselves) and a belief in 'constructive conflict' between individuals to generate value. They have never experienced effective team-working and only pay lip-service to the prevailing orthodoxy on the need for team structures and the value of teams.

Until their belief changes (which is likely only to occur through a personal and positive experience of the power of teams), their companies will not achieve as much growth as would be the case of there was genuine commitment to teams.

To quote Montebello and Buzzotta again: 'Teamwork is replacing the outmoded, adversarial approach that has grown between management and labour and that now threatens the competitiveness of many companies around the world'–but only when the key decision takers believe in teams.

As mentioned in the first chapter, I have tried to ensure that personal anecdote is kept to a minimum. I think I have been successful, and so shall share the reason why I am personally a passionate believer in teams.

Eight years ago, working for a previous employer, I had passed some tests and had been moved out of a subsidiary as a high-flier. I had been scheduled to attend a junior managers' intra-subsidiary team-building course, run internally at the organization's management training centre, before my promotion. As the bureaucratic process was fully in gear, there was no question of my withdrawal. Normally, when on training programmes with my peers, I had deliberately tried to shine and to beat the competition in a highly individualistic and egocentred way. Now I knew that I was the only high-flier, and I did not perceive any threat from my fellow course members. In advance of the programme, therefore, I decided to adopt a low key, even humble approach. For instance, during the programme, each of the three teams had to produce a video on improving an aspect of corporate communications.

Previously, I would have mentioned my thespian experience at school, and ensured I got a lead role in front of the camera. On this programme, with my team, I kept my mouth firmly shut and volunteered to be the camera man, and became the butt of some humour as I was not very good.

The fortnight was one of the best experiences I have had, not only because our team was the best performing team, but also because I learned so much from my team-mates, and we had so much fun. One fact stuck out, as it summed up the experience. Two of the members of our team had worked in the subsidiary I had but recently left; both knew me and had worked with me. At the end, they both told me that they had seen my name on the programme they had received in advance, and both had prayed devoutly that I was not going to be on their team. Their prayers were unanswered, but they had reversed their judgement at the end, because I reversed mine at the beginning.

Problems with teams

You have your own answers based on personal experience of working with groups. You may well find that most managers and executives have a similar set of problems. The list set out below is intended to be representative rather than exhaustive, and the pooling of the views of a small group of executives:

- Too much control by the most senior person present or 'leader'.

- Laziness by members of the group—a lack of commitment.

- Lack of decision-taking—a weak leader.

- Too much team-talk and not enough action.

- Poor group performance, feeling tarred by the group brush, especially when, as leader, you have gone along with the majority view against your better judgement, which turns out to be right.

- Poor time-keeping.

- Individuals creating their own power base and splitting the group.

- Relationships too cosy—a lot of humour, even frivolity, social chit-chat, but little focus on the task.

- Too much information kept within the group—not publicizing themselves enough nor sharing information with other relevant groups/ individuals.

- Individuals deliberately undermining the authority of a new leader.

- Your ideas having cold water poured on them by senior group members.

- Too conservative: individuals always carrying out roles they are comfortable with—no learning.

- Unsure of your own role, feeling isolated and excluded.

- Too much talking and not enough listening.

- Endless red-herrings.

- Not confident in carrying out role allocated—no support provided by other group members.

- No sense of direction nor purpose.

- Too much attention to procedure and detail.

- Too much action and fire-fighting and not enough thought.

- Hidden agendas, and behind the scenes manoeuvres.

- No agendas for team meetings.

- Having to sit through team meetings when your expertise/contribution was only required for a small part.

- Secretaries at meetings who were excluded or didn't want to be there.

- Too many people present.

- Insufficient expertise to complete the project/task properly.

Now, if we replace the problems with their opposites, we get a powerful model of effective team-work—a vision of what needs to be achieved, though not, as yet, a clear picture of how it is achieved.

So carrying out the reversal process we have a collective view that effective team-working comprises the following:

- Appropriate leadership (the nature of which is examined in the section 'Leading team growth').

- Enthusiastic, committed group members.

- Effective decision-taking.

- The proper balance between planning and action.

- Strong performance, with the right mix of technical skills.

- Strong creativity.

- A mutually supportive environment, but not too comfortable.

- Focus on task achievement, with clear agendas.

- Sharing information within the group and externally.

- Good listening skills.

- Individuals prepared to take risks, make mistakes and learn.

- Clarity of the role of each individual in the team.

- No hidden agendas: 'feelings on the table'.

- All members of the team involved and participating.

- The right number.

- Clear sense of direction and purpose.

Now that we have a view of what an effective team looks like, let us consider the phases a team passes through to reach the goal of effective team-working.

Team development

Please refer to Table 8.1. There are many models of team development, which the experts agree are very similar. There is a model, based on the work of B.W. Tuckman (1965), which defines four stages: cautious affiliation, competitiveness, harmonious cohesiveness and collaborative team-work. Another, developed by Psychological Associates has four similar stages: reactive (forming), authoritarian (storming), casual (norming) and true team-work (performing).

The model set out in the chart also has a number of similar stages, based on the reality of managerial and executive experience, but seeks to link in the impact of leadership style and relate to the concept we have already explored of the development level.

Table 8.1 Team development

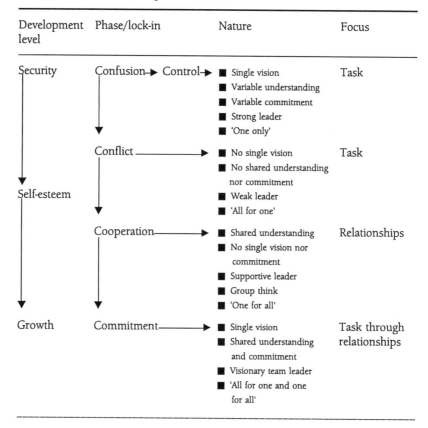

Development level	Phase/lock-in	Nature	Focus
Security	Confusion → Control →	■ Single vision ■ Variable understanding ■ Variable commitment ■ Strong leader ■ 'One only'	Task
Self-esteem	Conflict →	■ No single vision ■ No shared understanding nor commitment ■ Weak leader ■ 'All for one'	Task
	Cooperation →	■ Shared understanding ■ No single vision nor commitment ■ Supportive leader ■ Group think ■ 'One for all'	Relationships
Growth	Commitment →	■ Single vision ■ Shared understanding and commitment ■ Visionary team leader ■ 'All for one and one for all'	Task through relationships

Confusion

When a group forms, i.e. meets for the first time, the team itself will be at a low level of development. It will be immature. The individuals will be in a new, unfamiliar situation. As we have discovered, the impact of change, if sudden and even perceived as positive, can throw people out of balance. They can temporarily drop a development level. This is why I have called the initial phase 'confusion'. There is inevitably a high degree of confusion owing to unfamiliarity and uncertainty in the new environment.

People are concerned with themselves rather than with others—there is an ego-focus. They tend to be cautious, reserved and wary. They may be angry, unsure as to why they are there, what is expected of them—not wanting to be there. These perceive the change negatively. Others will perceive the change positively, but are likely to be impatient with the muddle and confusion, wanting structure and purpose and annoyed at its absence.

There tends to be little communication, lots of silence and unpleasant pauses. People are wary of making any commitment or exposing themselves to a group of relative 'strangers'. The group as a whole and the individuals are in high NC/LD mode.

At this stage, leadership becomes a vital issue. As we know, when we are in NC mode there can be a dependency on or need for a strong leader, to remove the uncertainty and provide direction and purpose. So what happens next will depend on whether there is a leader and what kind of leader there is. Usually, in work situations, there is a predetermined leader who has been given the positional power by the company. If there is a strong leader, then the leader will move the team beyond confusion into what I have termed the 'control' phase.

Control

This can be a permanent resting place for the team. They are locked into control. As a team they are operating at a permanently low level, which does not justify the team's existence. The team becomes an imperfect instrument to execute the wishes of the leader.

If the leader is just 'command and control', then we shall have the reactions described in Chapter 6. Some people will silently resist and play lip-service to the leader's instructions, and others will try their best to implement their leader's wishes but without full understanding. The team will be both inefficient and ineffective. If the leader has a strong visionary ability, then a more united team may emerge, a more effective instrument to execute the wishes of the leader. It cannot be an effective team, because there cannot be any synergy. There is no exploration nor discovery, no controversy nor debate.

In fact, the pure control outcome will only occur with a visionary leader. Even if the leader is authoritarian, some aspects of the 'conflict' phase will be permanently present, with little ability for any progression into higher levels of development.

The conflict phase will occur naturally with teams with no initial leader, or teams with a weak leader or teams with a leader who is not sufficiently strong to exercise total control or with the effective team leader, who is aware that a conflict phase is inevitable and needs to be entered and exited as quickly as possible.

Conflict

The best way to illustrate the conflict phase is by example: an artificial one, but one that illustrates the kind of behaviours and approaches that occur as the team develops.

Imagine a group of managers or executives who have been working together in a training environment for nearly a week, and have learned about how to develop teams and the different leadership styles that are appropriate. They have been put into an outdoor environment and are just about to start an exercise with which they are totally unfamiliar. Worse, they have been asked to put on blindfolds, and are standing rather nervously awaiting instructions. A piece of equipment is thrown into the centre and the tutor says: 'With the equipment provided, form a perfect square and place yourselves equidistant around it.' (The piece of equipment is a single long length of rope.) What do you think happens next?

While there are variations in behaviour and approaches, there are common themes. Very few teams indeed efficiently and effectively solve the problem, though most get there or nearly there after some considerable time.

- There tends to a rush for the rope—most are eager to get their hands on the problem and resolve the immediate uncertainty.
- The initial phase is dominated by heat and very little light. A number of people vie for the leadership role, and helpful suggestions by individuals are completely lost, e.g. 'shall we nominate one person to coordinate our efforts?' or 'let's not implement one idea before we have explored all the options'.
- The person, who can get the group to listen to his or her idea, tends to become the leader. Often the idea is modified or changed early on by someone else and that person takes over. Occasionally, when an idea has been agreed, another individual coordinates the implementation with the originator focusing on the technicalities.
- There usually comes a time when the majority are locked into implementing an idea, and any alternatives are dismissed.
- Clarity of communication is low because of an over-reliance on words, and often people are doing what they are told to do quite cheerfully but with no understanding of why.
- There is a lot of subgrouping with two or three talking to each other at the same time, with no cross-communication.
- One or two become completely turned off, just standing holding the rope, waiting for something to happen.
- Once everyone has got hold of a piece of rope, which happens early on, there is considerable reluctance to let go. Indeed, in most groups, only solutions which permit continuous holding of the rope by all members are implemented.
- Individuals can become quite dogmatic not only locking permanently into the 'one right answer', but also into a completely wrong answer. For instance, one individual in one group asserted strongly there were two ropes. This was accepted by the group as a whole and a solution developed, until the evidence against the proposition became overwhelming.
- However, most solutions involve activity by all towards the end. Then, individuals begin to believe they will succeed, energy levels and commitment soar and the end comes much more quickly than external observers anticipate. It is as if 90 per cent is spent in confusion and muddle, and almost magically a solution is achieved out of very little.

In the feedback and review sessions, where a process model is developed, the managers recognize that a lot of these behaviours occur from their experience in the workplace.

If we look back to the problems you and others have experienced with groups, many of these reflect the conflict phase, e.g.

- Confrontation and competition—vying for leadership if there is no appointed leader, or challenging the authority of the appointed leader.

- Laziness by members of the group—a lack of commitment.

- Poor group performance, feeling tarred by the group brush.

- Poor time-keeping.

- Individuals creating their own power base and splitting the group.

- Individuals deliberately undermining the authority of a new leader.

- Your ideas having cold water poured on them by senior group members.

- Unsure of your own role, feeling isolated and excluded, leading to opt-out.

- Too much talking and not enough listening.

- No sense of direction nor purpose.

- Too much action and fire-fighting and not enough thought.

- Polarization within subgroups and elements of in-fighting.

- A focus on task, but not on process nor relationships in the group.

- A lot of direction by one or two members, with one-way communication and little involvement.

- Anger and frustration at lack of progress.

As we see, many of us have worked in groups, where we spend most of the time in the conflict phase. However, just like individuals, teams rarely stay purely in one phase, as events, circumstances and tasks change. Like individuals, however, a team can have a strong orientation towards one development level or phase.

Teams with a strong leader will tend to stay in the control phase with aspects of conflict, and rarely progress unless the leadership approach changes. If the team has a weak leader with a task focus, then the team will be oriented towards the conflict phase, moving occasionally to the cooperative phase, where there is lock-in to the 'one right answer' by all the group and feelings of support emerge because of a unity of purpose in pursuing that answer. If the weak leader has a supportive aspect as well, then the tendency will be for movement between the conflict and cooperative phases. Conflict will resume, when the right answer is proved wrong or not as right as was assumed by all.

Cooperation

The cooperative phase, as we have seen with the rope exercise, often evolves in teams of peers with no formal leader. It is as if there is a psychological reaction to the explicit or implicit negative emotions occurring in the conflict phase. In fact, teams of peers with no appointed leader, where the individuals are known—such as a group of accountants, lawyers, managers or executives from the same firm or company—usually move swiftly to this phase. This is particularly true of informal settings with a social overtone like 'strategy events' or 'away-days'.

As mentioned, if there is a leader, and he or she is naturally relationship oriented rather than task oriented, then his or her group will spend a lot of time in the cooperative phase.

If we look back at the problems we see one or two which reflect the cooperative phase:

■ Endless red-herrings.

■ Too much team-talk and not enough action.

■ Relationships too cosy—a lot of humour, even frivolity, social chit-chat, but little focus on the task.

In the cooperative phase the focus is on relationships and not task, either as a reaction to conflict or as function of the composition of the group and the setting or as a result of the leadership approach. The result is what is termed 'group think' or 'one for all'. Individuals are reluctant to disturb the harmony by injecting controversy. If and when an idea or solution emerges, then everyone enthusiastically supports it.

The climate is very supportive, and there is a lot of team-talk with little decision-taking. Getting things done can take an age, as the group flows in one direction and then another—all together, but not focused on or committed to task achievement.

One major drawback to the cooperative phase is that it is difficult to progress into the final phase, because the group members think they are there.

Progression will be a function of the quality of leadership if there is a formal leader, or will depend on the extent to which individuals within the group without a formal leader know and share their knowledge about teams and how to develop the correct process and achieve synergy. The other way to develop a fully committed and effective team with or without a formal leader is to conduct a formal team-building event with an external facilitator, who is perceived as credible by all team members.

We have already considered what an effective or fully committed team looks like. Before considering how the team leader (assuming an appointed leader) can create growth, let us examine two examples of leadership style that lead to lock-in to different levels.

EXAMPLE

Margaret Thatcher is a classic example of a strong leader who produced lock-in to the control phase with aspects of conflict. Cabinet meetings were formal rubber-stamping affairs with the use of formal ministerial titles and predominantly one-way communication flows. All those who became 'one of us' tended to show various levels of commitment and understanding of the leader's vision and help the leader drive it through with a focus on task and not relationship! There was resistance, with hidden agendas and behind-the-scenes manoeuvres. Explicit disagreement was rare as the penalty was exclusion.

EXAMPLE

John Major is seen as a weak leader with strong relationship emphasis. This has produced periods of cooperative team-work with lock-in to the 'one right answer', e.g. Membership of the Exchange Rate Mechanism. Once events destroyed the answer, there was rapid deterioration into the conflict phase, from which movement was difficult with no single vision nor strong leadership to produce a control phase (where there is progress towards task achievement). What has tended to happen is for short-term 'one right answers' to emerge with short-term cooperation, destroyed by the events which prove those answers wrong.

There is another fundamental point, raised as one of the problems 'too many people present'. Effective team-work is impossible if the numbers are too large, as is the case with cabinets of 21. This unrecognized reality means that the full cabinet can only be a talking shop or a rubber-stamping device. Inner cabinets or one-to-one relationships with the leader and special advisers become the real decision-making units.

What is the right number to produce an effective team? If we take Professor Belbin, a name with whom some of you may be familiar, the answer is somewhere between four and eight. Professor Belbin has carried out years of research into and written about teams. He has identified eight team roles (Belbin, 1981):

1. *Shaper*: providing focus and shape to the team's efforts.

2. *Chairman*: coordinating the team's efforts.

3. *Plant*: providing the ideas.

4. *Monitor evaluator*: providing a critical, independent review.

5. *Company worker*: focusing on pragmatic reality and implementation.

6. *Resource investigator*: looking externally and bringing in information and contacts to the group.

7. *Team-worker*: providing support and care to develop cooperation.

8. *Finisher*: focusing on setting and achieving deadlines; getting the job done.

According to the professor, individuals will have strengths in one or more roles (which can be identified by a questionnaire), and an effective team needs all the roles present but no duplication to avoid clashes. The numbers of people are likely to vary between four (two different roles each) to eight (one different role each).

This approach and its conclusion are very interesting, but, in my view, constitute a too individualistic and static concept of an effective team. An effective team is a powerful learning vehicle for the individual, with the individual having the capability and need to become strong in a number of different roles. This is also a necessity as few teams are ever selected according to the Belbin model.

More importantly, everyone in an effective team is at least creative and supportive: it should never be the function of one person to suggest the ideas or provide the support.

The answer to the right numbers is determined by the limitations of effective work-roles (no one should be there to make up the numbers without a genuine contribution to achieving the task), and the number and clarity of work-roles, subject to an overall limitation, provided by the need for everyone to be involved, to participate and be committed.

The result will tend to be the same—between four and eight—but not always. There have been examples of footballers, rugby players and cricketers who have operated as effective teams. These teams are rare because of their size, but can occur because of the number and clear definition of work-roles—the positions the individuals take in the side.

Leading team growth

In this section we shall try to get a feel for the kind of leader who can build an effective team, and what that person needs to do to produce the magic synergy.

You may recall that in Chapter 6, 'Initiating change', when looking at persuasion I introduced the concept of visionary team leader, or VTL, derived from my earlier book on persuasion. This is an individual who, most of the time, can operate at the growth level of development. This is someone who first and foremost has a strong group orientation: believes in the team and knows how to produce synergy. There will be strong empathy skills: the ability to communicate effectively and get on well at the individual level; rational logic; and a low use of incentives and hence need for control.

Looked at differently, the VTL is the only leadership approach that can produce an effective team.

- If the leader does not believe in the value of an effective team, he or she cannot produce one. A leader without commitment cannot create commitment. Team members would instantly sense the lack of commitment, irrespective of what the leader said.

- If the leader does not know how to produce an effective team, the team won't be effective.

- If the leader is strong, whether or not driven by a personal vision that can be sold to the team, he or she can only produce a team that is mainly locked into control or conflict, or a combination.

- If the leader is weak with a task focus, the group will spend most of its time in the conflict phase.

- If the leader is weak with empathetic skills, then the team will move between conflict and cooperation as events and circumstances unfold.

- If the leader is highly empathetic and supportive, then the cooperative phase will predominate.

If the logic is accepted, then there is one conclusion for companies wanting to produce growth out of change: produce a culture of VTLs through training and development of all those in leadership positions!

Now before we look at how the VTL can create an effective, committed team operating at growth level, let us return to the subarctic and the question posed:

'What does the group need to do, how can it achieve it and what behaviour/ approaches should individuals adopt to guarantee the creation of synergy?'

Answers from different groups are surprisingly similar. One set comprised the following:

What?

- Ensure that individual views are expressed and information is shared.

- Manage time.

- Ensure that ideas are brought out and developed.

- Ensure that specific expertise is identified and expressed.

- Decide rationally on the basis of the facts identified and knowledge developed.

How?

- Appoint a member of the group to coordinate the group's activities–to manage the process agreed.

The individual

- Have an open mind.

- Have good listening skills.

- Question assumptions (own and others) and be assertive.

- Be non-competitive and committed to the goal.

- Be prepared to change your mind in the light of new information.

- Stay committed if in the minority and a decision is taken on the basis of the majority view and not a real consensus.

Realities

A number of interesting realities occur in this synergy exercise:

- The very act of thinking constructively about synergy increases the probability that it will be achieved. Even in a very short time, positive behaviours and actions are induced by the explicit consideration given.

- A very high level of synergy is created in a short time where these approaches are successfully adopted.

- The greatest drawback to synergy is competition in the group. On one occasion, two 'experts' had had solo journeys in difficult terrain, and the group had enormous negative synergy, i.e. each individual would have had a greater chance of survival if he or she had acted alone and not been part of the 'team'. The two 'experts' disagreed furiously and the rest of the group could make little or no effective contribution.

- Decisions based purely on majority voting do not produce synergy. There has been no generation of new knowledge.

- It is psychologically very difficult to stay committed when your views have been overturned. This reduces synergy considerably, as the group either loses the enormous potential value of one individual who opts out, or is subject to an *agent provocateur*.

The emergence of 'group think' denies a significant degree of synergy. Quite often, especially with peer groups who know each other, there will be a small degree of overall synergy and there will be one individual who has significantly outperformed the others. This begs the question as to why this individual did not assert his or her views, and the reasons behind them and why no one paid attention.

The answer is usually a reluctance by the individual to disturb the comfortable atmosphere and he or she will accept any rebuttal immediately. Effective teams operate with a delicate balance between challenge and support. Hence the need for open minds and good listening skills as well as individual assertiveness, based on acceptance that the facts and reasons of any assertion will be uncovered and challenged, which is critical to the development of new knowledge.

The purpose behind our brief consideration of synergy is that this knowledge is part of the repertoire needed by the VTL when developing team growth. When considering what a VTL needs to do to develop a team, I have made the assumption that the group is meeting for the first time, and so will be in the confusion stage of development. The model is set out in Figure 8.1.

Explicit management of expectations

As we have seen in the last chapter, the explicit management of expectations is critical to gaining positive outcomes in relationships whether internally or externally. The team is no exception. There are four key aspects to be covered.

Acknowledge reality

You, as VTL know (though the team does not know that you know) the feelings and uncertainties that they have as well as the kind of behaviours they are likely to demonstrate in the absence of your proactive intervention as a visionary team leader. It is highly empathetic to acknowledge the reality of those feelings and uncertainties *though not the possible future behaviours*—to let them know that you understand and appreciate where they are coming from. It has an immediate positive impact on their attitude to you as leader, and helps you gain the respect of the group. Team members respect a leader who respects them.

You should not mention likely future behaviours as that gives a negative mindset and, paradoxically, gives permission for them to occur. More importantly, your proactive management will reduce if not eliminate those behaviours and enable substitution with the positive behaviours and approaches that are required for synergy.

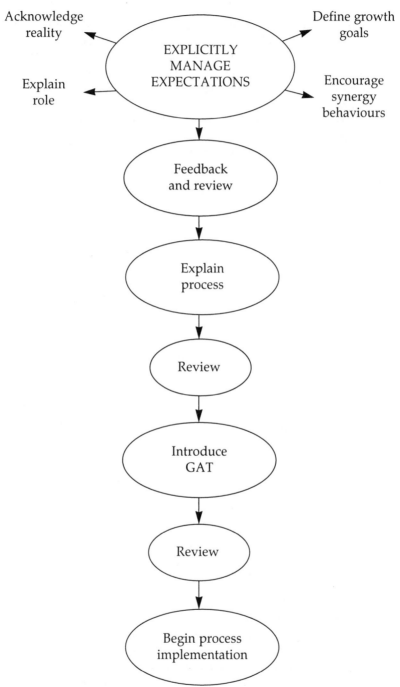

Figure 8.1 *Leading team growth.*

Authority is not required by a VTL, but respect is. You are, in fact, exercising a considerable degree of control in the initial phase, as this is necessary for development. But it is control through care: caring for individual wants and through the focus/development of individual needs, which will be satisfied by the 'commitment' team. The purpose of the control is not to get your own way, so the nature of the control is different.

You will find that you will learn as you lead. You have to have all the behaviours and approaches of the individual, operating effectively to generate synergy in a group. The difference is that you bring these behaviours and approaches to the team as a key component of your leadership skill. You then demonstrate them to help create them in your team members.

Define growth goals

Most leaders focus on the task at an early stage. You are a visionary team leader. Focus on the task comes later. You focus initially on the team, which is what you are developing; so:

- *Set out the goal for the team*: i.e. to be a highly motivated, supportive group of individuals committed to a shared vision of what needs to be done and how it can be achieved.

- *Explain the reasons*: i.e. the team will be more efficient and effective than the sum of the contributions of individuals acting in isolation. This will have highly positive outcomes of improving business performance and enhancing the company's perception of the competence of each individual.

- *Use a 'group' persuasion approach*. Emphasize that the achievement of these highly desirable outcomes is not the task of one individual (yourself as leader) but of every individual in the team. 'All of us need to work together to achieve the goal.'

- *Ask for feedback*. There is rarely verbal dissent, as the goals are 'noble' and no one likes to be seen as disagreeing with them. Remember that the group is in the confusion stage, and there tends to be silence, so do not expect anything more than a nod and a 'yes'. In the early part of your leadership, you may find yourself ploughing a lonely furrow. Don't be put off. It doesn't last very long, and when the ice is truly broken you will be delighted with just how positively and rapidly matters progress. By asking for feedback, you are setting the example of a critical component of effective team-working–feedback and review. You are beginning to establish the right group norms.

Encourage synergy behaviours

It is worth referring not merely to what the team is aiming for as its growth goal, but also to some of the requirements of all individuals to achieve synergy—open mind, good listening skills and so on. Some leaders set out a list of ground rules to which they ask the group to commit themselves. This tends not to work very well as it is too prescriptive at such an early stage and tends to receive standard 'confusion' phase responses.

Other leaders carry out the first group exercise where the team decides the ground rules that will bind it. This works better, but could be seen as occurring too soon and without the group atmosphere that GAT produces (once the technique has been effectively introduced). I favour the helpful suggestion rather than the ground-rule approach, but this is a matter of leadership style.

One other thing I would mention is that if you believe in the power of humour to generate both strong group cohesion and a high degree of creativity, that 'behaviour' should be explicitly mentioned and encouraged.

Explain role

All team members are concerned about their new leader, and usually find out what kind of leader that person is only by what he or she does or does not do. As a VTL, guesswork can be removed by explaining that your role is to help develop an effective team and to *initially* manage the process whereby the team tasks are achieved.

You may be surprised by the use of the word 'initially'. At the heart of effective leadership, whether of an individual or a team, is the need to adopt an approach that meets the requirements of the individual/team and the particular situation or task.

If we take the process of effectively delegating a new task to an inexperienced follower, then, as we saw in Chapter 6, we need to use the leadership approach that moves from a high level of initial guidance and control to a more supportive coaching approach as competence and confidence grows. Eventually, we shall be the infrequent 'questioning coach'—very much removed from the task itself.

When teams have reached their growth level, our leadership role changes. At the growth level, all the individuals in the group have the capability of carrying all the team-leadership roles necessary—such as process management or leading a review or GAT. In fact, some companies use the VTL to develop growth level teams who become self-managing teams. The VTL is removed from the group as that person's task is done.

With a designated leadership position ordained by the company and accepted by the team, this is not practicable, but increasingly the VTL becomes one of a mature, united cohesive group of competent individuals rather than a *primus inter pares*. The VTL no longer 'leads from the front'. A good VTL produces a team of VTLs.

Explain process

Periodic times for review are essential to confirm understanding and allow individual views to be expressed and explored, and these have been built into the model.

There is not a totally defined process for task or project completion, and it is a matter to be explored by the team. However, there are common elements in any effective process management and it is worth sketching out an initial process model, which forms the basis for subsequent action. It is a necessary part of removing uncertainty and providing direction and focus.

A task process is set out below:

- Share information

- Distil key points

- Clarify and confirm nature of task

- Agree objective/first milestone

- Develop time plan

- Carry out GAT

- Evaluate options and agree actions

- Agree work-roles (subgroup and individual work) and resource requirements

- Agree initial phase and first deadline

- Set time for feedback and review

- Agree time-outs

- Execute first phase

- Feedback and review

  and so on.

Key points are:

- Information is power, and critical to 'empowering' the team is sharing information and leading the process of distillation of the key points— scoping the project or task.

- With the development of the GAT approach, the level of contribution and involvement will be very high at a very early stage.

- Regular, structured feedback and review are essential to ensure that the project stays on track or that the need for a change in direction, if necessary, is identified and pursued as soon as possible.

- Breaking down the task or project into discrete chunks with interim deadlines and milestones will enable any performance or resource problems to be identified and remedied quickly, as well as ensuring that motivation remains high because there are short-term goals to be met, and not just some long-term distant objective.

You may have noticed this strange phrase 'time-outs'. The concept recognizes the reality that a focus on relationships and emotions in the context of the task will enable the development of an effective team. If there is purely a task focus, then aspects of the 'conflict' phase cannot be avoided. They can be significantly reduced by building in the rule that if any individual is feeling uncomfortable or upset, then he or she can call a time-out during which the group as a whole considers and resolves the issue.

When looking at perception gaps, we recognized that more often than not problems and conflicts between individuals were not the result of a conscious effort to hurt or humiliate, but were caused accidentally by not noticing or considering the impact of what we said or did, or simply by being carried away by our own emotional reactions to change and stress situations.

Even with the positive impact of the VTL, 'personality' clashes and negative emotions and reactions will take place. The more individuals can be encouraged to 'put their feelings on the table', the less they will fester and the more quickly will a positive cooperative approach be developed.

Introduce GAT

Having explained the process model and received feedback, a very powerful way of creating the atmosphere that helps deliver the 'commitment' team is to introduce GAT, if not a cultural norm. As mentioned in Chapter 7, it is best to only try out a few humorous or non-task related issues at this stage.

Once the laughter has died down, the final act of the VTL in the pivotal deployment of his or her role—the initial stage—is to commence process management. Only now should the focus on task achievement begin.

Impact of change and reality

In this final section, we examine some of the realities of teams in the working environment and how we can best deal with them as VTLs.

Implicit in looking at teams and team development has been the assumption that the composition of the team is unaltered during the completion of the task or project. That is increasingly less and less the case. So we look at change in composition, both temporary and permanent, as well as change in the task, and the impact of the unexpected.

Change in composition

Temporary

Even with project teams or departmental teams, there will often be occasions where one or more members of the full team are absent from team meetings, whether sick, on holiday, or unavailable because of pressures of work they are doing in their other purely individual roles, unrelated to the team task or project.

The impact, without effective management by the leader, knocks the team down from effective performance or 'commitment' to cooperation. There is an automatic move towards group think at the meeting, with potential for further downward movement towards conflict when the absent members return if they have not been fully briefed. *All for one and one for all* cannot be sustained automatically if the 'one' and the 'all' have changed. However, as group norms of behaviour and support have been established, conflict is unlikely at that meeting.

The VTL needs to recognize this. The best policy is to try to ensure full attendance at meetings by all the team. But, as reality dictates, this will not always be the case, and the leader needs to ensure that:

- A full brief has been received from the absent members as to progress in their areas of task or project responsibility.

- The team is fully advised.

- If they have particular roles in terms of the team process and dynamics, these are allocated to the leader or other team members. Incidentally, this exemplifies the power of a GAT approach. If there had been a reliance on the Belbin type individual team role, there could be insurmountable problems: for instance, if the creative 'plant', on whom the team relies for ideas, is absent, where do the necessary ideas come from? With the GAT approach, there is not much difference between six people thinking creatively together and seven.

- There is an early review to regain task focus under the new conditions.

- The absent individuals are fully briefed after the meeting (preferably in person by the leader) on decisions taken and the reasons, particularly where additional work has been 'allocated' to them during their absence!

Permanent

If one or more team members leave permanently without replacement, then the process is similar to that just described, except there will also need to be an agreed allocation of task or project duties. Clearly, effective action should be taken to reduce the non-team workload of those with additional responsibilities (if significant), otherwise team performance may be diminished by the stress of individuals who are overworked.

When there is an additional member or replacement, there will be an immediate regression from 'commitment' to conflict. Hence, for instance, the covert or explicit undermining of a new leader, mentioned earlier in the problems with groups. Not only is the task disrupted and the shared vision broken, but there is an 'alien' in their midst. The tendency, if the new member is not the leader (and in the absence of effective intervention by the leader), is for the group to either explicitly advise the new member of 'the way things are done here' or let that individual learn 'the hard way' all the group norms that have been established. There is an inevitable closing of ranks as the existing members react by moving into NC mode against the uncertainties generated by the new arrival.

If there is a new team member, then the existing leader needs to recognize and stop this reaction by starting the team development process all over again!

It is a little bit more difficult for a new leader. Remember the 100-day rule: A new leader should not initiate change for 100 days, but just listen and observe. The new leader will then appreciate the valid reasons for not making some of the changes that he or she initially contemplated. Initiating change can then be done more effectively, because the changes are connected to the present and the past, which is now understood.

There is also one other reason for delaying the team development process. This is to allow the NC reaction (which will occur against the new leader but will be expressed in much more subtle ways because that person is the leader) to reduce or be eliminated as the team realize that the leader is not a 'command and control' merchant and also realize that he or she appreciates what the team do and why they do it.

However, 100 days will be unnecessary. That period is predicated on the fact that the new leader was not a VTL.

Change in task

Commitment teams will often degenerate to conflict when there is a new task or project. I have seen it so often: previous success guarantees future failure. A new project may well require a new task process, and will always require different tasks as well as a level of technical competence or knowledge that is not currently available within the team. There are also the 'uncertainty' and 'unpredictability' aspects of change, which lie latent, concealed by the over-confidence of the successful team, convinced it can conquer Everest. There are inevitable mistakes or failures which produce a conflict reaction as they represent a change that is significant, unexpected, sudden and perceived negatively!

Teams can be broken by success.

If the leader recognizes this reality, then he or she must ensure that the group returns to the beginning of the task process: sharing information, defining the new task and agreeing the objectives, agreeing the overall process, carrying out GAT, allocating new roles, and so on.

Built into the process will need to be time to develop the required level of technical competence or knowledge before implementation.

The unexpected

No team operates continuously at commitment level, once reached, during a project, even if there is no change in members or if any change is effectively managed by the VTL. This is because of the 'unpredictability' aspects of change.

CASE STUDY

A group of executives were carrying out a complicated computer-based business simulation. They had reached commitment level, having effectively digested the brief, devised their strategy, and made good policy decisions. They had input their decisions into the computer for the first two rounds and the results exceeded expectations. They were all gathered round the computer, having just input the decisions for the third round. Disaster! They made a huge unexpected loss. I have never seen such a rapid descent into conflict. Within minutes, after the shock had been absorbed and accepted, the tutors had been blamed for a stupid simulation, the sales director and production director were having a stand-up row, each blaming the other, the finance director was in a corner pouring over the printouts, the personnel director had disappeared and the MD was a helpless spectator!

Now disaster on this scale may not strike, but the unexpected and negative invariably will. This is why time-outs can be so important. It also shows why teams, if they are going to gain maximum performance, need an individual (whether a nominated leader or another team member) who has the authority to manage the process. A process manager is always required at all times.

Assuming the leader has this role, then he or she will need to move swiftly into 'control' mode, and call a time-out, so that soothing oil is poured on emotionally troubled waters before leading a GAT-type meeting where the causes of the problem are identified in a rational manner and solutions put forward and accepted. It is important that this is a team-based activity, even though the crisis occurs at subgroup level.

Key point summary

- Research indicates numerous benefits to be derived from team-working such as improved quality and productivity, employee motivation and commitment, and customer satisfaction.

- Companies which implement a policy of training team leaders to build effective teams will generate the full benefits to be derived from team-working.

- The core value to a company of an effective team is that it produces better results more quickly than the individuals could achieve working separately. The effective team produces synergy, which is a powerful means of creating growth from change: managing difference for value.

- Companies will not get the best out of teams unless the top decision takers have experienced effective team-working and so are committed to creating a team-oriented culture.

- The value to the individual is that the team is the most powerful vehicle for individual growth and learning.

- When teams are not performing well, there can be a host of problems, varying from too much control to too little, from poor decision-taking to none at all, from lack of commitment to too much socializing, too much focus on procedure and detail, lack of vision and sense of purpose, time-wasting and so on.

- Effective teams have committed enthusiastic members, involved and mutually supportive, strong creativity, a shared sense of purpose and direction, and a focus on task achievement.

- Teams pass through a number of levels of development or phases, before achieving synergy. They can become locked in one phase or move between lower levels of development, not justifying their existence.

- When teams form, the initial phase is *confusion*, characterized by feelings of uncertainty among team members, a focus on self, and a degree of caution and wariness. There will be either annoyance at being involved or impatience at the lack of structure, clarity of direction, purpose and individual role, depending on whether the individual perceives the change negatively or positively. The confusion phase is marked by little communication and lack of commitment.

■ With a strong leader, the team will move into the *control* level, where it may rest permanently if the leader has a powerful vision to which the team becomes committed. The team becomes a willing instrument of the leader's wishes. There is no synergy, as there is no discovery.

■ With a 'command and control' leader there will be aspects of the *conflict* phase as well as control. There will be a natural progression to the conflict level for teams with a weak leader or no formal leader. This phase is characterized by challenges to the leader or for the leadership, subgrouping and opt-out, poor time-keeping and group performance. There is negative synergy and no shared vision nor sense of direction.

■ As a reaction to the conflict phase, marked by negative emotions, or as the result of the efforts of a supportive leader, teams move to the *cooperation* level, where the relationship side is developed, producing camaraderie and mutual support. The focus on task–a characteristic of the earlier phases–diminishes and 'group think' emerges: slow progression along different routes at different times, with complete agreement after lengthy discussion or 'team-talk'.

■ The ultimate level is the *commitment* level, where the team is united, task-focused and produces synergy. To achieve this level requires a visionary team leader (VTL) if there is a formal leader, or knowledge in a self-managing team of how to achieve commitment–shared among the group and acted upon.

■ The right group numbers for an effective team vary between four and eight, and can be a little higher where there are a sufficient number of clearly defined separate task-roles for each individual in the group. With larger numbers, there cannot be effective participation and involvement by all.

■ The VTL requires the same skills as the QC (questioning coach), but with the added dimension of commitment to the team concept, coupled with understanding of how to build effective teams.

■ When leading a newly formed team towards commitment level, the VTL needs to:
 —manage expectations explicitly through acknowledging the reality of the feelings of the new members, defining the team goal of effective

performance, explaining and encouraging the behaviours and approaches that effective teams demonstrate, and advising in the personal role of team leader;

—explain the task process, subject to review and change to be agreed by the team;

—introduce the GAT (group action thinking) technique;

—commence process management after feedback and review.

■ Where there is a temporary or permanent change in the composition of the team, a new project or task, or the inevitable, but unexpected setback during a project or task, the team will inevitably regress, usually down to conflict. The leader needs to recognize this reality and proactively manage the team back to commitment level by restarting the development process (new member), restarting the task process (new project) or calling a 'time-out' to settle the relationships in a GAT-type problem identification and solving session (unexpected setback).

■ With a commitment team, the leader will become indistinguishable from any other team member, i.e. all members become capable team leaders and can manage the process. However, there always needs to be a process manager (whether the same or different individuals over time) to take control when a change disrupts team performance.

Your own points

Your action plan

Growing the organization

> *I now know how little I know about running*
> *businesses.*
>
> CHRISTOPHER RODRIGUES, CEO of
> Thomas Cook
> (said to the troops after attending a
> Global Leaders Programme)

Introduction

In this final chapter we concentrate at the organizational level, focusing on the top executives. As said in the Preface, they have the power to create or deny the development of an environment or culture in which change is accepted positively as the norm.

We start by looking briefly at *culture*, a word that is becoming universally used in the context of the effective management of change. We then consider two important issues that need to be addressed before the top team can take the reins into their hands. Finally, we examine what research has to offer, focusing on what the executives need to do to ensure that their organization creates growth from change. In the process, the key themes from earlier chapters are pulled together.

Culture

To introduce the concept, let us eavesdrop on a conversation between a junior person and a very senior person in a company. The situation is that of an up-and-coming high-flier, John, working as an assistant manager in market research, whose boss, Tessa, is the head of research. Tessa's boss in turn is Harry, the head of the marketing department, and his boss is the sales and marketing director, Charles.

John had done a few ad hoc projects for Charles directly, initially because he was the first person Charles had got hold of, and subsequently because John had done excellent work the first time round.

Charles had just finished briefing John on another little project. Then, out of the blue, as John was about to leave, he said: 'I like you, lad—you remind me of myself 25 years ago. So I am going to give you some sound advice, which I suggest you listen to and follow.'

'Oh, thank you, Charles,' replied John.

'Now, you believe, don't you John, that if you perform very well you will be promoted, and that if you continue to perform well and exceed what this organization expects of you, you will continue to be promoted? In other words, you believe that good performance is the key to a successful career?' Charles asked.

'I do, indeed Charles.'

'And why do you believe that, John?' This director was very good at promoting discovery with people he liked.

'Because that is what I have been told, Charles—what is more, the appraisal system is structured to measure and reward performance, and everyone these days is appraised by their boss. And also, that has been my experience. To date, I have performed very well, and I have been promoted.'

'I see, John, that is a bit of a worry. You may be right in the early days of your career, when you are still junior, but those days are over. You are now completely wrong, and I want you to understand this so that you have the effective career your talents deserve,' remarked Charles.

'Well, I hear what you say, Charles, but I am afraid that I do not really understand why you say what you say.'

'I know, lad,' commented the director. 'Let me explain. Every organization has a culture, the way things are done round here, if you like. There are always two sides to the cultural coin—the light side and the dark side. You are operating at the moment purely in the light side. Unless you learn to walk in the shadows—in the twilight zone of the culture—you will fail in your career ambitions.'

'I see, Charles,' said John. In fact, he didn't see anything at all! He was in his own little twilight zone. 'Could you be more specific, please?'

The director chuckled at John's obvious discomfort. 'The twilight zone is all to do with human nature and particularly its frailties. If you like, the explicit or light side is where our hopes and aspirations lie. The implicit or dark side is where our less noble natures express themselves. For instance, on the light side we might say and believe that feedback is good. So we say to new recruits that we encourage an open, honest atmosphere of two-way feedback between the boss and subordinate.

'On the dark side, where reality, not aspiration, lies, if you were to directly criticize your boss, Tessa, for instance, who might be directly criticizing you all the time, you would probably destroy your career. She would not take kindly to criticism from a subordinate. If it became a habit, she might not tell you off, as she might not like direct confrontation. What she would do, almost inevitably, is to ensure your appraisal did not reflect your performance, and she would be very lukewarm indeed in supporting you, when it came to promotion.

'Take another of so many examples. These days, we promote creative thinking, as our industry is at the forefront of change, and ideas help us to

manage change effectively. So we encourage ideas on the light side of the culture, but not on the dark side, especially from juniors like yourself, unless they are purely focused on completing the task that you have been given or you are asked to come up with ideas, which hardly ever happens.

'On the dark side, if you were to suggest to your boss, Tessa, for instance, that she takes on board a good idea you have, then you will be seen to be criticizing the current way she does things. Now she is responsible for the status quo, with which she will often personally identify. An idea necessarily suggests a difference to the status quo. So, by expressing an idea, you could be and often will be seen by many bosses as criticizing them even though that is not your intention. So, you have fallen into the dangerous trap, by coming up with an idea, of criticizing your boss—not a career progressive move.

'Do you begin to understand, John?' asked Charles.

'Yes, Charles, I am beginning to see the light, or is it the dark?' replied John.

'I'll forgive that attempt at humour,' smiled Charles. 'Let me make it more personal. You have done some excellent work for me recently, and I bet you think that it has enhanced your career prospects. In fact, you may well have been boasting a bit to your colleagues about this.'

John looked a little bit sheepish, but said nothing.

'You couldn't be more wrong, I'm afraid. Unwittingly, I have done you a disservice. Let me ask you a few questions. Did you consult with Tessa and ask for her input and advice before giving anything to me, having clearly briefed her on what I wanted you to do and why?'

'No, I didn't,' said John. 'Though a few times she was not around.'

'But you could have written to her, and kept her informed that way, could you not?' Charles continues probing.

'I could have, but I didn't because I didn't see the need', came the reply.

'OK. Did you brief her afterwards, feed back the results of our meetings?' asked the director.

'No, I did not,' replied John.

'Well, look at it from Tessa's point of view and my point of view. You are so far removed from me that I do not take decisions on your career. If I were to take decisions at your level, I would spend almost all my time doing that. That is not my job. My job is to ensure that the sales and marketing division meets its targets, and help steer, together with my colleagues on the board, the corporate ship to a safe harbour.'

'Of course, I understand that,' acknowledged John.

'Now, your boss, Tessa, knows all about the twilight zone. It is important that she pleases her boss, and she is very keen to make a good impression with me. She is one step closer to me than you are. So I have a little bit more impact on her career. More importantly, if I like her and think she is sound, I might drop that piece of information to the personnel director

when we are chatting, as we often do. Even more importantly, she is due for promotion, and if she gets Harry's job (and Harry, as you know, is retiring in a few months) then I become her boss, and therefore a very important person indeed.'

'I understand that, Charles.'

'Now how do you think your boss feels about your activities? She sees you getting much more direct access to me than she does, she sees you in my confidence where she is not, she sees you keeping her in the dark completely, and, for all she knows, deliberately.'

'She is not going to be a happy lady, at all.'

'And, who is she going to blame for this highly negative state of affairs? Me, a very important person in her eyes, or you, a very unimportant person in her eyes?' persisted the director.

'Well, me of course. But why hasn't she spoken to me?' asked John.

The director laughed uproariously. 'There is one golden rule of the twilight zone. No one ever speaks about it. You only learn the hard way. Good God, man, do you know anyone who would deliberately and openly say such things as "I'm an insecure, petty, jealous person, who resents you for what you are doing, even though it is not your fault"? Enough, John, here endeth your first and I would imagine your last lesson on the twilight zone.'

Implication

There is always a twilight zone in any organization, but whether the gap between 'light' and 'dark' is or remains large will depend on whether it is recognized by decision takers and whether the structures and systems that are put in place encourage staff to actually do what they may all verbally agree should be done for organizational success. This key point is developed in the final section, expanding on the research findings from Warwick University.

It is very interesting to note the specific findings of Roger Harrison (1991), who has produced a culture questionnaire, examining levels of consciousness in an organization.

Very broadly, irrespective of the level in the hierarchy or the country of origin of the company, the results are the same: the culture is seen to be operating at a mix of security and self-esteem development levels (a low level of consciousness), and a mix of self-expression and growth (or a high level of consciousness) is desired.

We all seem to desire the right things for personal and organizational growth, but few are able to deliver what we all desire.

Key precursors

Structure and roles

Boards have a number of executive and non-executive directors. Within the executive side, there may be a single leader—a combined chairman and chief executive officer—or a separation of the two roles. Shareholders increasingly do not like the concentration of power in one hand, and prefer a separation of 'executive roles'. A recent case in point was Barclays Bank, where the shareholders forced the separation. A number of issues arise at board level:

■ What is the role of the board (with non-executive directors) as compared to the executive team, which may contain executives who are not board members?

■ Assuming a separation of the roles of chairman and CEO, who is responsible for what?

■ If team-work is accepted as the most powerful way to manage change for growth, who is the team leader and what is the team?

These are fundamental concerns. In the absence of an effective resolution, the top of an organization will be permanently in conflict and/or control mode. The consequences will be:

■ With weak leadership, an organization will be engulfed by the short-term, permanently reacting to the changing external environment, and permanently in fire-fighting mode. The top will either tend to become unwitting upholders of organizational inertia and resistance to change, or subject to fits and starts—different directions and strategies emerging at different times as change is driven from below, and power passes over time to different power centres within the organization.

■ With strong leadership, there will be far too much of the 'uncertainty' aspect within the dilemma of change—an attempt to impose or inspire a single direction to a defined future, which is doomed to fail in the long term.

Conventional wisdom has the board as the representative organ of the shareholders, through which the chairman is held to account. Additionally, the board is responsible for the formulation of strategy, and monitoring the implementation. The implementation of strategy is managed by the executive arm.

Reality tends to be that the executives actually carry out both the formulation and implementation of strategy, and effective accountability to the board is non-existent or minimal. The reasons are:

- Information is power. Information resides with the executives who are running the company. The statutory duties of boards require the usual excess of information, mostly of a non-strategic nature. There is little strategic information available to non-executive directors, from which strategies for change can be formulated by the board as a whole.

- The chairman/CEO combination (whether one or two people) holds the power at board meetings. The chairman chairs the meeting in which he or she is supposedly to be held to account.

- Meetings of the board are formal and infrequent. Even if the numbers were right, effective team-working is not possible, so there cannot be effective change management by the full board.

- Selection of non-executive directors is often made *de facto* by the chairman. With strong leaders, particularly, this results in non-executive directors who are 'one of us' and become instruments in the implementation of the leader's vision.

Is there a way forward that will ensure structures, roles and approaches that increase the effectiveness with which the top of organizations manage the change process?

Clearly, if you, the reader, are a board member, you need to ensure that these issues are recognized, raised and discussed so that the people involved discover and solve.

Putting on a 'teaching' hat, some suggestions are:

- Reduce the size of the board to no more than eight. This is in fact a general trend, already well established.

- Separate the roles with a non-executive chairman who is recruited from outside the company for a fixed term, not a company individual who is getting old or has lost a power battle and has been 'kicked upstairs'.

- Recognize reality. Make the CEO (and the executive team) responsible for the formulation and implementation of strategy, with accountability to the board, led by the non-executive chairman.

- Ensure that 50 per cent of the board are non-executive directors, again recruited by the board for a fixed term from outside the company, or even industry. Continuity can be retained by staggering the start date for individual non-executive directors.

- Introduce a greater frequency of board meetings and a separation of purpose, one set for regular review and discussion of strategy, and the other set to fulfil statutory requirements.

Ants and elephants

Executives are increasingly recognizing the need for clarity of role to avoid turf and power battles, as well as the power of the team to deliver added value and strategic focus. This change in perception is usually the result of a learning experience involving all the top team.

What they also realize, and this is applicable to many companies and individual executives, is that they are in a strait-jacket—they are not addressing the right elephants and are spending too much time killing ants, which produce little meat for the table.

The ant is a trivial work-activity—a meeting, a phone call, an information flow, a project and so on that does not add value. An elephant is a core business goal, the achievement of which does add value. The elephant can be broken down into measurable objectives, and into activities or tasks that result in the achievement of those objectives. So, if developing clients is a core goal for us, those activities that help us to achieve the objective of increasing our client base by 10 per cent in a year are elephant activities.

A generic problem for almost all executives is that they spend too much time dealing with ants and not elephants.

There are two factors at play.

1. The team as a whole spends too much time dealing with issues that should be delegated to the individual functional or line executive member.

2. The individual line or functional executive spends too much time focusing on his or her own area of responsibility. Often the individual has been promoted with little knowledge and skill in carrying out a strategic, future-looking role, and is comfortable with his or her area of expertise.

Invariably, the precursor to effective change management requires us to:

■ Introduce informality, e.g. away-days to help develop a team atmosphere and allow the team members to get to know each other as people. (I have often been told by members of top executive teams that the emotional side is taken as read or unnecessary to consider as everyone is deemed 'mature'. The result is an exclusive focus on task, which guarantees that the 'team' is permanently in conflict or control mode with all the power-plays and subgroupings that guarantees. A classic case of a false implicit assumption of 'maturity' that was never identified.)

■ Re-focus meetings to consider strategy and change as a priority.

■ Reduce the time the team spends on managing the present—focus on feedback and review meetings, predicated on the assumption that the line and functional executives can do their job.

■ Ensure that individual executives delegate, to their line managers, responsibility for the day-to-day implementation of strategy. This usually requires some sort of training of those senior managers, so that they can be comfortable with and capable of exercising their greater autonomy and authority effectively.

Once these changes are in place—and for many companies they never happen because there is no recognition of need—then the management of change for growth can begin.

Managing change for growth

The book closes with the fruits of research by the Centre of Corporate Strategy and Change, Warwick Business School. The research is summarized in Table 9.1 and in this section each aspect is examined and linked back to earlier chapters. The focus is on the role of those with the power to ensure that the processes of change are effectively introduced.

Creating momentum

Real or constructed crises to overcome inertia

A wise leader does not wait for a real crisis, but generates a perception of crisis, based on exaggeration of those trends emerging that have a negative implication. As mentioned in the first chapter, a jolt to the system is required to overcome inertia and create a perception of the need to change.

At present, real crises are very frequent, and often act as the spur. The problem is that change is best managed if there is a certain slack in the system, and profitability and cash-flow are favourable to make the investment that change requires. If you are hit by a sudden crisis, as occurred at IBM or ICI, then the negative path of the reaction curve is deeper and more painful—and for some there is no other side.

This is why strategic thinking—the ability to question, analyse, exercise judgement and get the timing right—is so important for the leaders of today. There is always a recipe for success, if only it can be uncovered. The problem is that the recipe can be changed by market forces, and no one may notice.

Let us consider a couple of cases.

Table 9.1 Summary of research on managing change for growth

Creating momentum	Sustaining momentum	Critical success factors for long term
■ Real or constructed crises to overcome inertia	■ Consistent and persistent drive from the top	■ Flexible means
■ Champions and teams to lead change	■ Marry top-down pressure and bottom-up concerns	■ Managing succession
■ Generate challenge, risk and unlearning	■ Develop islands of progress and publicize success	■ Coherence in the management of the overall processes of change
■ Create broad visions and not blueprints	■ Ensure zones of comfort and relative continuity	■ Creating a continuous process view rather than an episodic view of change
■ Alter the management process and structure	■ Provide freedom to customize within the broad vision	
■ Generate power shifts and learning from doing	■ Allow opportunism	
■ Focus	■ Deal with dead-ends and remove blockages	
■ Rethink and reshape information flows	■ Refashion reward and recognition system	
■ Use deviants and heretics	■ Change knowledge and skill base	
	■ Find and use role models	
	■ Build capacity for change in non-receptive areas	

CASE
STUDY
When Lou Gerstener was made CEO of the card division of American Express in 1977, he was told that the price of the product was too high and the market was mature. Yet for 12 years, until he left, his division enjoyed continuous profitability—with profits more than quadrupling from £7 million to £30 million. He discovered a simple recipe for success, which lasted a very long time:

- Focus on a consumer segment with a higher income, and appeal to their desire to be differentiated: 'You are privileged and special people with a privileged and special vehicle to demonstrate that reality.'
- Meet their needs: remove hassle, and ensure a reliable, secure and widely acceptable product.
- Develop a wide network of establishments, keen to give higher discounts to attract prestige clients.

The recipe was baked into a profitable cake through developing people, deploying systems and the intensity of Lou's drive and commitment.

Eventually, competitors caught up, as Amex forgot the need to revisit the recipe—keep it accurate, crisp and clear.

CASE
STUDY
IBM had a recipe for success in 1984, and yet failed to notice that there was an irreversible structural shift in the market, entirely predictable in 1984 but not predicted by IBM!

The IBM recipe was: 'Technology driven, with proprietary technology, mainframe, hardware—a box, sold through the IT director, who also bought personal computers for his or her professional staff.'

Thanks to the survival of Apple and the drive of Steve Jobbs, the new recipe comprised:

- Microprocessing power—driving enhanced performance at lower cost and enabling miniaturization.
- The personal computer as the new force, with a wider range of users, different buyers—marketeers and business users (most hiding from the IT director!) and different buyer behaviour—software solutions to business needs!

IBM died in 10 years.

Champions and teams to lead change

There need to be individuals at the apex of the organization who recognize the need to change, and are committed to achieving change—but they cannot achieve it alone. They need to build teams. This has been a key theme. Effective teams obtain value from difference—and difference is the heart of change.

Generate challenge, risk and unlearning

Clearly, part of the old must be swept away: a cultural shift is required so that 'thinking outside the box'–challenging conventional wisdom–is encouraged, ideas flow more freely and risks are taken. In a world of change, mistakes become the stepping stones to success and not the dole queue.

However, so often, in the past, attempts to change have floundered on the corporate and individual mindset–the 'not invented here' syndrome. To learn requires unlearning–sweeping away the cobwebs that cover the ceiling and deny recognition that it is in fact the sky.

Some organizations have made unlearning a core principle of change management. They burn before they build: they sacrifice the 'sacred cows'.

You may have come across the concept of 'zero-based budgeting', which has progressed to the grander 'business process re-engineering'. The concept, whether applied purely to budgeting or to the business as a whole, is to start with a clean sheet, assume that what is in place does not exist and rebuild according to the goals determined appropriate to the changing future.

It can be a very painful process. Unless commitment to it is gained, and unless there is time spent in the visioning process so that employees believe in the vision and the goals derived from it, then the reaction curve is guaranteed for many employees, because many are hit by sudden change, which is perceived as negative.

Additionally, much of what was worth keeping lies in the ashes of the past.

If there is little belief in the need for change by the mass of employees, then this approach can be the necessary jolt to the system, but it requires careful management and maximum employee involvement.

It does have the significant merit, however, of focusing on the future rather than dwelling in the past, or trying to quantify the present to such an extent that there can be no long-term growth in the future.

If we focus on the planet Earth, can we ever reach the stars? It is interesting to note that the Japanese giants–Sony, Mitsubishi, Komatsu, Toyota, Cannon, Daichi Kangyo–were but tiny stars in the industrial firmament 20 years ago. If they had focused on their performance and capability at that time, they would still be where they were. Rather, they looked to the long-term, set themselves a long-term strategic goal or statement of intent, then shorter-term *corporate challenges* to ensure focus and to provide the stretch that is at the heart of real achievement.

Create broad visions and not blueprints

This is at the heart of changing for growth–recognizing both the need for some overall sense of purpose to inspire and unite, and that competent confident people like to 'do their own thing' once they have an overall context for decision-making.

Too often the blueprint approach is taken, especially to quality, where process and procedure rather than principle and purpose dominate the agenda, producing robots who leave their imagination and souls at home.

Alter the management process and structure

As implied in the section on culture, you cannot change culture without changing structure. At the heart of culture is people and the environment in which people develop is largely affected by the management style they receive.

Many organizations are increasingly trying to develop cultures, which enable delivery of a quality service or product that meets customer needs or solves their problems.

A few have recognized what this actually means in practice, and are endeavouring to grasp the nettle. They are attempting to reverse the organizational pyramid. They have identified that current structures and management processes will deny the cultural shift they desire.

Given the reality of the 'dark side' of the culture, staff focusing on pleasing their bosses, so that they focus internally and upwards, will not simultaneously be able to focus outwards to the client base.

These organizations are therefore reversing the role of boss and subordinate—no longer servant but master, no longer master but servant. To achieve this, the key shift is in appraisal systems, which encapsulate the power of the relationship. They are being reversed from downward appraisal to upward appraisal.

This is a brave experiment indeed, but there are enormous dangers. Culture produces conformity, as organizations sideline or sack those who do not conform.

People become set in their ways as their expectations, attitudes and behaviours have become normalized over a narrow spectrum. To achieve reversal effectively means an enormous investment in training and development so that staff are effectively empowered—i.e. can handle competently and maturely the freedom they are being given—and managers can adjust to move from 'command and control' or 'control and support' to 'questioning coach'.

I don't think these organizations realize the sheer scale of disruption and pain that will be caused, or the unexpected depth of the reaction curve unless the change is sold effectively and made progressively, gently and by means of pilot and then gradual implementation.

More importantly, it is unnecessary, if there is recognition of the power and value of a team approach, so that the base structure is a team one, and appraisals are equalized rather than reversed. They are carried out on a mutual and team basis. This is particularly necessary if we remember that, in an effective team, all are equals with simply the role of process manager required.

Generate power shifts and learning by doing

Machiavelli stated that agents of change receive the implacable hostility of those who perceive themselves disadvantaged, and only lukewarm support from those who perceive benefit.

This reality not only requires 'champions and teams' but shifting personnel, eliminating those whose hostility cannot be overcome and promoting those who are positive and proactive. In a sense, there is no gain without pain, though pain should be minimized so that gain in the long term can be maximized.

Too much planning leads to paralysis from analysis. Change requires experimentation, and there is a need for immediate pilots and projects to develop learning from doing, and to start creating momentum with the mindset that 'change is the only constant'.

Focus

As Brian Pitman, of Lloyd's Bank, said: 'Strategy means focus and hard choices.' We achieve if we focus. This means that there should be focus on the change process itself, but also a sequential approach to implementation: focus on one or two 'change challenges' at a time and over time and not implement too much too quickly.

Rethink and reshape information flows

Information may be the life-blood of an organization, but many are finding that their arteries are becoming hardened by an excess of information and data flows, a situation compounded by the advent of networked systems.

Knowledge is power and the free flow of knowledge, essential to any networked organization, will create organizational power or organizational learning. As Peter Senge (1990) wrote in his seminal work, *The Fifth Discipline*: 'Organizations will only survive in the future if they learn at a pace that is faster than the pace of change in their environments.'

If this is true, and it makes sense, then only a networked organization where there is a free flow of knowledge can become a 'learning organization'.

But who ensures that knowledge is transmitted? At the moment it tends to be pure information or data, interpreted differently and individually. Charles Handy (1985) and Peter Drucker (1967) have both stated that successful organizations of the future will incorporate 'knowledge workers', whose role is to analyse and interpret data and information to produce meaning and knowledge, which is then transmitted. So, for instance, the accounts are interpreted and analysed and the key learning points distributed. The accounts themselves form merely an appendix into which only the true *afficionado* will bother to dip.

Use deviants and heretics

The age of the rebel has dawned! Good leaders recognize that the culture must change and that 'deviants and heretics'—those who have been crying in the wilderness—have insights and ideas that are vital to effective change management.

Sustaining momentum

Consistent and persistent drive from the top

There should be delegation of implementation, but never abdication of management of the overall change process, which is eternal.

Marry top-down pressure and bottom-up concerns

New communication channels need to be developed: team briefings, videos, newsletters, weekend seminars off-site, and so on. Continuous communication and feedback are vital. Visibility and managing by walking about become a core task of the top. When I listened to General Sir Peter de la Billière recently, he emphasized how critical in the Gulf War it was for him to be visible and to communicate to the troops—and that is what he spent a lot of his time doing.

Initially, as we know, change produces discomfort and uncertainty. Visibility and communication are vital in calming the nerves and developing understanding and empathy.

Develop islands of progress and publicize success

Focus on initiating change early through pilots in areas where it is most likely to succeed. It is like sitting an exam: always go first for the question you can answer well to build confidence and generate momentum from success.

The imagery of a majestic galleon sailing at an even pace through the calm waters of change is a false one. Rather there is a flotilla of little boats, storm-tossed with some being sunk by the waves, and a few forging ahead acting as beacons to the boats struggling in their wake. The leader's lights should shine brightly in the dark.

Ensure zones of comfort and relative continuity

There must be land to look back on and recognize. Change should be a narrow isthmus and not a vast ocean. That is at the heart of continuous improvement: once you have undertaken that necessary shift in direction, you can always recognize where you have come from as you move forward.

Provide freedom to customize within the broad vision

A theme already developed.

Allow opportunism

As a necessary strategic response to the unpredictability aspect of change, the culture must accommodate those who remain rebels. The leader must be able to say to the rebel: 'You want it, you go for it. These are the boundaries and here are the resources—and remember to stay in touch.' That is the role of the scout, and is vital when undertaking a voyage of discovery. The scout may find a corner to cut or a crevasse to avoid, or may die.

Deal with dead-ends and remove blockages

Boats that are wallowing badly need to be rescued swiftly or the plug pulled for a quick, clean and permanent submergence. If the net becomes entangled, it should be disentangled at once or the catch will be lost. Momentum must be maintained.

Refashion reward and recognition system

The values, attitudes and behaviours required to make the broad vision or dream a reality will not be achieved unless the dark side of the culture is significantly diminished.

We have seen how change in structure and management processes is necessary. These must be complemented by compatible changes in reward and recognition systems. They are part of the 'incentives' aspect of persuasion. So if you want a continuous improvement culture, you must reward continuous improvement in the areas where improvement is desired. This means abandoning rewards based on the achievement of quantified results. If someone is rewarded on completing a project by a specific deadline, there is no incentive to improve that project continuously!

Equally, if your goal is to achieve a team-based culture, then reward the team, not the individual.

Change knowledge and skill base

In an environment of change, we are all more unconsciously incompetent than we think we are. So learning is the key to getting growth out of change. It is only when leaders like Christopher Rodrigues recognize they need to learn, and enjoy an effective learning experience, that they recognize that this is a permanent reality. The very act of experience and recognition gives the organization led by such individuals a competitive edge.

Part of the Japanese success story is predicated on this knowledge. They have the Zen approach to training: training is a continuous process throughout the working life. Its purpose is to enlighten the individual as well as help the organization.

The West has tended to have the Confucian approach to training: training is to prepare for promotion. So once you have reached the top, you don't need to learn!

Edward de Bono exemplified this on a seminar I attended. He was talking about six-hat thinking, a very powerful process that can help a positive cultural shift towards more efficient and effective thinking. He remarked that he had a breakfast meeting with the chairman of Nippon, the Japanese communications giant. The purpose was to discuss how this thinking process could be introduced company-wide. De Bono mentioned that he could not imagine having such a meeting in the West.

Once the top recognizes the need to learn, then the knowledge and skill base of the organization as a whole can be radically improved.

Find and use role models

The champions of change should inspire others to follow in their wake: let the beacons of the leading boats burn brightly.

Build capacity for change in non-receptive areas

This is crucial. If there are too many laggards, and too many boats that are wallowing or holed below the water-line, the momentum of the flotilla as a whole will be destroyed. The beacons of the leading boats may burn brightly but to little avail if they cannot be seen!

Action will usually revolve around people—to be developed or replaced, but there may also be the issue of connection. It will often be the case that vessels find themselves being steered in directions that are eventually outside the broad beam the vision provides. If that is the case, then they can simply be let go.

Critical success factors for the long term

Flexible means

It is a function of size (and successful growth guarantees increasing size) and a function of time for there to be a lurch towards the 'uncertainty aspect of change'—i.e. for too much rigidity to slip into the system.

Additionally, success breeds complacency, a natural antidote to continued renewal. New ways soon become old ways, which become the accepted best ways and ossification creeps in. All the evidence shows that organizations have a natural tilt towards 'inflexible means to a defined end'. This means that flexibility of means must become a strategic goal in its own right.

Managing succession

The leader of the leaders—the overall champion of change—must be replaced by someone who has the same understanding and commitment to change and all that change entails.

Too often, experience of the task is the criterion for selection and not understanding of the process.

Coherence in the management of the overall processes of change

This theme was introduced in Chapter 1: it is the processes of change, not strategy, that must be understood and managed in a world of change.

Creating a continuous process view rather than an episodic view of change

Put simply this means that the organization, the teams and the starting block—the individuals—need to develop a positive attitude to change, recognizing it as the new norm and welcoming it, because they have benefited from it. They know that the more change there is, the more they will develop.

If change is managed badly by the top and the middle, the bottom will be wearily waiting for this nasty episode in their lives to finish, so that they can return to the 'good old' days. That is why some organizations are putting the client to the top and reversing the pyramid, so that staff learn to serve the customer, helped by their former 'bosses'.

Personally, I believe in mutual assertiveness with clients and staff, based on the reality and equality of the effective team.

Epilogue

'Delight' is better than 'satisfaction', and delight comes from a shared voyage of discovery ... and now this particular voyage is over I hope I have achieved my goal of helping you create growth from change.

Rupert Eales-White

The Persuasion Inventory

You have been asked to complete the enclosed 'inventory' or set of statements which determine the approach to persuasion of the individual who has given the inventory to you. It will take about 20 minutes, and there are only three requirements:

1. You should answer from the perspective of your relationship with that individual and your knowledge of how she or he operates in the working environment.

2. You should be totally honest, and try to avoid thinking and analysing too much—go with your initial, instinctive response.

3. Consider each statement, and if you agree more than disagree, tick the A box. If you disagree more than agree, tick the D box. For each of the 80 statements a decision is required.

He or she ...

	A	D
1 promotes creative thinking	☐	☐
2 cares about colleagues' feelings	☐	☐
3 regularly checks that members of staff do what they say they will do	☐	☐
4 uses facts and logic to persuade other people	☐	☐
5 enjoys a good argument	☐	☐
6 disciplines a member of his or her staff who makes mistakes	☐	☐
7 believes team working is the way to benefit from different individual approaches	☐	☐
8 finds time to listen to colleagues' concerns and problems	☐	☐
9 appeals to the company's vision and values to persuade another	☐	☐
10 gives emotionally more than he or she receives	☐	☐
11 believes that getting the facts right is vital to persuading another person	☐	☐
12 is quick to praise another for good performance	☐	☐
13 considers rewards and punishments to be an effective way of persuading another	☐	☐
14 holds strong views and opinions in most matters	☐	☐
15 is trusting and trusted	☐	☐
16 ensures that targets, objectives and performance standards are agreed by team as a whole	☐	☐
17 ensures that his or her staff know what is expected of them	☐	☐
18 thinks analysis and logic is the way to solve problems	☐	☐
19 ensures that most decisions are taken by the team as a whole	☐	☐
20 recognizes the need to understand and respond to others' points of view before persuading them to his or hers	☐	☐

He or she ...

A   D

21 believes that success in persuasion will come from getting the facts right and building up a strong, logical case ☐ ☐

22 keeps his or her staff under control ☐ ☐

23 paints an exciting picture of future possibilities rather than concentrating on present realities ☐ ☐

24 provides emotional support to colleagues ☐ ☐

25 easily handles any challenge to his or her views ☐ ☐

26 prefers to be part of group creativity sessions rather than thinking creatively alone ☐ ☐

27 believes that work is only effective if there is a solid structure and discipline ☐ ☐

28 has well-developed listening skills and is a good listener ☐ ☐

29 is quick to criticize others when they make mistakes ☐ ☐

30 listens more than talks when with another person ☐ ☐

31 will hardly ever alter a previous decision if sure of the facts ☐ ☐

32 deploys key corporate objectives, such as having a client focus, when persuading someone ☐ ☐

33 is convinced that he or she usually has the right answer ☐ ☐

34 tries to motivate individual members of the team by developing shared goals and common values ☐ ☐

35 finds that if the staff are told exactly what is required and why, they will agree to do it ☐ ☐

36 respects colleagues and is respected by them ☐ ☐

37 puts forward strong logical arguments in discussions ☐ ☐

38 lets members of staff know how their performance will be measured ☐ ☐

39 coordinates rather than controls the team ☐ ☐

40 finds that by listening to and understanding another's position, his or her own initial stance is modified ☐ ☐

He or she ...

		A	D
41	uses authority to ensure that staff meet their targets	☐	☐
42	tries to develop a caring and supportive environment	☐	☐
43	believes that having a genuine debate or dialogue with another is the way to effective persuasion	☐	☐
44	is a creative thinker and enjoys sharing and developing ideas with others	☐	☐
45	uses authority to provide necessary discipline	☐	☐
46	prefers working in a team than on his or her own	☐	☐
47	prefers to talk about his or her views rather than listen to others talking about theirs	☐	☐
48	listens to and understands people, who hold a different view	☐	☐
49	puts the interests of others first	☐	☐
50	won't be persuaded unless the other person has carried out thorough research	☐	☐
51	believes that, when necessary, the judicious use of threats will get agreement	☐	☐
52	focuses on the goals and values of the group to persuade an individual member	☐	☐
53	persuades others with the use of his or her authority and appropriate rewards and punishments	☐	☐
54	promotes not just own ideas and suggestions but also those of colleagues	☐	☐
55	encourages individuals in the group to share their feelings and expectations	☐	☐
56	has deep convictions and beliefs on what is right and how things should be done	☐	☐
57	enjoys developing knowledge through researching facts, logical thinking and analysis	☐	☐
58	provides regular feedback to his or her staff on their performance	☐	☐
59	believes that the outcome of a persuasion situation is that both parties should feel they have benefited	☐	☐
60	persuades individuals in the group to share information and support each other	☐	☐

He or she ...

		A	D
61	likes to be in charge	☐	☐
62	responds to the need to be sensitive to colleagues' feelings	☐	☐
63	considers that it is important, when persuading another, to develop knowledge through rational debate and logical discussion	☐	☐
64	helps others create a shared vision and understanding	☐	☐
65	listens to and comforts a colleague who is upset	☐	☐
66	prefers working with a team than with an individual	☐	☐
67	disciplines poor performers	☐	☐
68	believes that people let you down, facts don't	☐	☐
69	appeals to shared values and a common purpose when persuading another	☐	☐
70	finds that flattery often works	☐	☐
71	pushes his or her views strongly	☐	☐
72	promotes others' ideas ahead of his or her own	☐	☐
73	usually carries out communication and feedback in a team context	☐	☐
74	hardly ever changes his or her position on major issues or problems	☐	☐
75	makes staff aware that what is said is meant, and that they should do what is requested	☐	☐
76	openly expresses own thoughts and feelings and encourages members of staff to express theirs	☐	☐
77	believes that the best agreement is when both sides win	☐	☐
78	sets goals and targets to motivate his or her staff	☐	☐
79	is more logical than creative	☐	☐
80	is a catalyst and facilitator rather than a commander of the group	☐	☐

Recommended reading

Adair, J. (1988) *Effective Leadership* (rev. edn), Pan, London.

Back, K. and Back, K. (1982) *Assertiveness at Work*, McGraw-Hill, Maidenhead.

Belbin, Meredith R. (1981) *Management Teams: Why They Succeed or Fail*, Butterworth–Heinemann, Oxford.

Biddle, D. and Evenden, R. (1988) *Human Aspects of Management* (2nd edn), Institute of Personnel Management, London.

Blanchard, K. and Johnson, S. (1983) *The One-Minute Manager*, Fontana/Collins, London.

Buzan, T. (1989) *Use Your Head* (rev. edn), BBC, London.

de Bono, E. (1982) *Lateral Thinking for Management*, Penguin, London.

de Bono, E. (1987) *Six Thinking Hats*, Pelican, London.

Drucker, P. F. (1967) *The Effective Executive*, Heinemann Professional Publishing, London.

Eales-White, R. (1992) *The Power of Persuasion: Improving your Performance and Leadership Skills*, Kogan Page, London.

Erikson, E. (1959) *Identity and the Life Cycle*, International University Press, New York.

Fisher, R. and Ury, W. (1986) *Getting to Yes: Negotiating Agreement without Giving in*, Hutchinson Business, London.

Handy, C. (1985) *The Future of Work*, Blackwell, Oxford.

Harris, T. A. (1973) *I'm OK–You're OK*, Pan, London.

Harrison, R. (1991) *Humanizing Change: A Culture-Based Approach*, Harrison Associates, USA.

Harvey-Jones, J. (1988) *Making it Happen: Reflections on Leadership*, Fontana/ Collins, London.

Henry, J. and Walker, D. (1991) *Managing Innovation*, Sage, London.

Hermann, N. (1988) *The Creative Brain*, Brain Books, Lace Lure, North Carolina, USA.

Herriot, P. (1992) *The Career Management Challenge: Balancing Individual and Organisational Needs*, Sage, London.

Honey, P. (1980) *Solving People-Problems*, McGraw-Hill, Maidenhead.

Hunt, J. (1981) *Managing People at Work: A Manager's Guide to Behaviour in Organizations*, Pan, London.

Mackay, I. (1984) *A Guide to Listening*, Bacie, London.

Maslow, A. (1954) *Motivation and Personality*, Harper & Row, New York.

McCalman, J. and Paton, R. (1992) *Change Management: A Guide to Effective Implementation*, Paul Chapman, London.

Montebello, A. and Buzzotta, V. (1993) 'Work teams that work', *Training and Development Journal*, March 1993, American Society of Training and Development Inc., Alexandria, USA.

Parikh, J. (1991) *Managing Your Self: Management by Detached Involvement*, Blackwell, Oxford.

Pease, A. (1981) *Body Language: How to Read Others' Thoughts by Their Gestures*, Sheldon Press, London.

Peters, T. (1987) *Thriving on Chaos: Handbook for a Management Revolution*, Knopf, New York.

Peters, T. (1992) *Liberation Management*, Knopf, New York.

Pettigrew, A. (1988) *The Strategic Management of Change*, Blackwell, Oxford.

Scott, B. (1987) *The Skills of Communicating*, Gower, Aldershot.

Senge, P. (1990) *The Fifth Discipline: The Art and Practice of the Learning Organization*, Doubleday, USA.

Tuckman, B. W. (1965) 'Developmental Sequence in Small Groups', *Psychological Bulletin*, USA.

West, M. and Farr, J. (1990) *Innovation and Creativity at Work: Psychological and Organizational Strategies*, Wiley, New York.

Whitmore, J. (1992) *Coaching for Performance: A Practical Guide to Growing Your Skills*, Brealey, London.

Index